PENGUIN BOOKS

GETTING READY TO NEGOTIATE

Roger Fisher is director of the Harvard Negotiation Project, Samuel Williston Professor of Law, Emeritus, Harvard Law School, and coauthor of the international bestseller *Getting to Yes: Negotiating Agreement Without Giving In*. He is also a founder and active member of Conflict Management, Inc., and the nonprofit Conflict Management Group, two consulting organizations devoted to strategic advice and negotiation training.

Danny Ertel is a founding partner of Vantage Partners, LLC. Prior to founding Vantage, Mr. Ertel headed up the Latin American Practice at Conflict Management, Inc., was a Senior Researcher at the Harvard Negotiation Project, taught negotiation at the University of Toronto Law Faculty, practiced law with Debevoise & Plimpton, and served as a law clerk to the Hon. Justice Harry A. Blackmun on the U.S. Supreme Court. Mr. Ertel's first book, *Beyond Arbitration* (1991) (with Ferrara) was selected by the CPR Legal program as the winner of its 1992 Book Award. He is also the co-author, with Roger Fisher, of *Getting Ready to Negotiate* (1995), and editor of *Negociación 2000* (1996). A leading authority on negotiation, relationship management, and conflict management, Mr. Ertel has written for, or been quoted in the *Harvard Business Review*, the *Sloan Management Review*, the *Economist*, *Purchasing Today*, and *Financial Executive*, among others. Mr. Ertel is a graduate of Harvard College and Harvard Law School, where he was Managing Editor of the *Harvard Law Review*. Mr. Ertel is also CEO and Chairman of Vantage Technologies, a company focused on creating enterprise software that leverages the consulting tools and expertise of Vantage Partners.

Conflict Management, Inc. (CMI), acts as an advisor to and trainer for organizations and individuals on negotiation and on the process by which they manage critical external and internal relationships. CMI provides training, facilitation, mediation, and dispute resolution services to its clients throughout the world.

Roger Fisher and
Danny Ertel

Getting Ready to Negotiate

THE *GETTING TO YES*™ WORKBOOK

PENGUIN BOOKS

PENGUIN BOOKS
Published by the Penguin Group
Penguin Group (USA) Inc., 375 Hudson Street, New York, New York 10014, U.S.A.
Penguin Group (Canada), 90 Eglinton Avenue East, Suite 700, Toronto, Ontario,
Canada M4P 2Y3 (a division of Pearson Penguin Canada Inc.)
Penguin Books Ltd, 80 Strand, London WC2R 0RL, England
Penguin Ireland, 25 St Stephen's Green, Dublin 2, Ireland (a division of Penguin Books Ltd)
Penguin Group (Australia), 250 Camberwell Road, Camberwell, Victoria 3124,
Australia (a division of Pearson Australia Group Pty Ltd)
Penguin Books India Pvt Ltd, 11 Community Centre, Panchsheel Park,
New Delhi – 110 017, India
Penguin Group (NZ), 67 Apollo Drive, Rosedale, North Shore 0632, New Zealand
(a division of Pearson New Zealand Ltd)
Penguin Books (South Africa) (Pty) Ltd, 24 Sturdee Avenue, Rosebank,
Johannesburg 2196, South Africa

Penguin Books Ltd, Registered Offices: 80 Strand, London WC2R 0RL, England

First published in Penguin Books 1995

26 27 28 29 30

Copyright © Conflict Management, Inc., 1995
All rights reserved

ISBN 978-0-14-023531-9

Printed in the United States of America
Set in ITC Garamond Light
Designed by Kate Nichols

ACKNOWLEDGMENTS

No project like this is the work of just two people. We could never have created this workbook without the help, support, and encouragement first and foremost of our families, friends, and clients. Many people have read this manuscript, and many more have read *Getting to Yes*. From our conversations with people from all walks of life who took the time to share their thoughts with us on one manuscript or the other, we learned a lot about what was missing in those pages, and what would make this workbook a worthwhile addition to the tools that help busy people do good and do well. In particular, we want to thank all of you who served as guinea pigs with early versions of our various forms and examples. You know who you are, and in these pages you see the fruits of your efforts.

In addition, and just as important as the help we received from those who do not do this work for a living, is the assistance and advice we received from our friends and colleagues at the Harvard Negotiation Project, CMI, and CMG. The help we received from each and every one of our colleagues was selfless and invaluable. Every chapter we circulated for comments came back with thoughtful queries, useful ways to rethink or reframe an issue, and encouragement to continue. And, as in every situation, there were a few people who played relatively larger roles who we would like to specially thank. They are Scott Peppet and Drew Tulumello from Harvard, and Heather Meeker Green, Melannie Merkau, and Liliana Zindler from CMI. Without their willingness to help get things done under difficult conditions and during several late nights, we could have never completed this project.

Roger Fisher
Danny Ertel

CONTENTS

Using This Workbook

CHAPTER 1

Introduction

Why a workbook to help people prepare for a negotiation? *Getting to Yes* was published more than a dozen years ago. It has sold millions of copies. Yet even its readers and fans tell us that they often feel uncomfortable and uncertain about how they negotiate; the process is sometimes stressful and the outcome worse. They know how a negotiation *ought* to go, but they can feel ripped off and pushed around, or they might agree to something that is worse than it should be, damaging relationships along the way. Perhaps they should have walked out and gone somewhere else, but they did not know when to leave or where to go. These are some of the symptoms that inspired us to write this book.

Diagnosis: unprepared

Whatever kind of negotiation we face—from an internal office problem to an international sale, from seeking a raise to buying a business, from dealing with a union to dealing with the Russians—lack of preparation is perhaps our most serious handicap. This is true whether the negotiation is ongoing or has not yet begun, and no matter how much experience we have. In fact, the more experienced we are, the greater the risk that we fall into an established preparation routine that takes little account of the particular people with whom we are dealing or the particular problem with which we are confronted.

At Conflict Management, Inc., and Conflict Management Group (two consulting firms formed to take the concepts and tools of the Harvard Negotiation Project out to the world of business and public policy) we have consistently found that one of the most powerful things we can do to help negotiators get good results is to help them prepare more effectively. We have found this to be true when working with people in businesses, governments, guerrilla groups, and labor unions.

Why are negotiators unprepared?

People assume "just talking" is low risk

Sometimes we may think that preparation is unimportant. Since we know that we cannot be forced into an agreement, we see little risk in saying, "Let's hear what the other side has to say." If we like it, we can accept it. If we don't, we can walk away. Over the years, however, we have seen that the risks of being unprepared are high. How will we know whether we should agree unless we have some precedents or other benchmark for evaluating the agreement? How will we know whether to walk away unless we have some idea of how well we can expect to do elsewhere?

Perhaps more important, by being unprepared we surrender initiative to the other side. We lower the possibility that we can come up with some good ideas and arguments that will quickly solve the problem to our mutual satisfaction. We deprive both sides of our creativity.

"Preparation takes too much time"

Preparation does take time—but it probably saves more time than it takes. A well-prepared negotiator can narrow the issues for agreement, formulate elegant options, or evaluate tentative offers far more quickly and wisely than a negotiator who does not know the terrain. On average, we think that you should spend as much time preparing as you expect to spend in face-to-face negotiation. Certainly, some matters are trivial and neither deserve nor require much preparation. Others, however, involve high stakes, multiple issues, and perhaps several parties. In such cases extensive preparation is a good idea. Whatever the situation, spending time on preparation is likely to save time in the long run.

People don't know how to prepare well

Many people feel prepared if they know what they want and what they'll settle for. But if our preparation consists of creating a wish list, with a minimum fallback position, the only thing we will be ready to do in the negotiation is to state demands and make concessions. Positional preparation leads to positional negotiation. By focusing on what we will ask for and what we will give up, we set ourselves up for an adversarial, zero-sum kind of negotiation. But this kind of preparation often prevents us from finding creative solutions that expand the pie before splitting it, or from working side by side to solve some joint problem.

Positional preparation is the greatest source of stress and anxiety during negotiations. We might think that if we invest time and energy planning our demands and concessions we will feel more confident as we make them. But the reality of the matter is that a positional negotiator, even one who has thought about what positions to take and what concessions to make, has little basis for deciding when to make a concession. Making a concession when the other side won't simply rewards their bad behavior. Yet not making one can precipitate a contest as to who can be more stubborn. Preparing only by making a list of demands and concessions is preparation for a bad negotiation.

A systematic approach to preparation

Experience demonstrates that preparation benefits from a systematic approach. That is where this workbook comes in. To be well prepared, we want to get our hands around the entire negotiation, use a checklist to identify those areas where preparation is likely to be most helpful, and then get to work. Here is a system we suggest you use until you develop one that works better for you.

There is no single right way to organize ideas. We have developed over the years what we call "theory for practitioners"—concepts and tools that help busy people organize and clarify their thinking about negotiation.

Goal: a good outcome

A good result of a negotiation can be seen as involving seven elements. The better we handle each element, the better the outcome:

Interests   Whatever our demand or "position" may be, we and others involved in the negotiation would like an outcome that meets our underlying interests—the things we need or care about. The more we have thought about our interests in advance, the more likely we are to meet them.

Options   A good outcome should be among the best of all possible ways to deal with our differing interests. By options we mean possible agreements or pieces of a possible agreement. The more options we are able to put on the table, the more likely we are to have one that will well reconcile our interests.

Alternatives   A good outcome should seem better than any alternative away from the table, better than things we might do by ourselves or with others. Before we sign a deal—or turn one down—we should have a good idea of what else we might do.

Legitimacy   We do not want to be unfairly treated, nor do others. It will help to find external standards that we can use as a sword to persuade others that they are being treated fairly and as a shield to protect us from being ripped off.

Communication   Other things being equal, an outcome is better if it is reached efficiently. That requires good two-way communication as each side seeks to influence the other. We want to think in advance about what to listen for—and what to say.

Relationship   A good outcome will leave our working relationship strengthened rather than damaged. Preparation can help us think about the human interaction—about the people at the table. We should have some idea about how to build a relationship that facilitates, rather than hinders, agreement.

Commitment   The quality of an outcome is also measured by the quality of the promises that are made. Those commitments are likely to be better if we have thought in advance about the specific promises that we realistically can expect, or make, during or at the conclusion of a negotiation.

We have found that just about everything we would like to know in advance of a negotiation can be discovered by thinking about these seven elements. They provide a checklist, an organized way of diagnosing an upcoming negotiation, and a way of preparing for it. By thinking about each of these elements—the building blocks of a negotiation—we can get our "arms around the problem." That will enable us to go into a negotiation well equipped to produce a good outcome, or, if we can't, know when to walk away to something better.

How to use this book

The more familiar you become with this book, and with your upcoming negotiation, the easier it will be to make good use of the concepts and tools. Even if you are a stranger to both, the book should quickly become a comforting guide. To get you started, here are four suggested ways to proceed.

1. First, read straight through

Finish reading this introductory material and then continue straight on through the basic seven chapters without stopping to fill out any forms. This will give you a good idea of what is here and how it might prove helpful. Then come back to the **Priority Prep** section beginning on page 12, identify some key elements for your preparation, and fill out the forms for the elements that match those priorities.

2. Sudden prep

If time before an upcoming negotiation is short, if the substance is of limited importance, and if you would like a little quick help in getting ready, turn to the **Sudden Prep** form on page 11.

3. Priority prep

Jump right into analyzing your upcoming negotiation with the **Priority Prep** questions in the section beginning on page 14. In the light of that diagnosis, decide which elements are those to which you should give priority attention, and fill out those forms. Preparation is not simply a one step process. Between meetings, or during breaks, you may want to revisit this workbook, especially if new or unforeseen difficulties have come up. The tools in this workbook can help you organize your thinking at each stage of a negotiation.

4. Full preparation

Work on all the elements, filling out the forms in chapters 3 through 9. Our advice would be to move back and forth among the forms, working first on the material with which you feel most confident and identifying other points on which you may need research or assistance.

Ultimately, the best preparation checklist or method is the one you prepare yourself. This workbook—with its maps, tools, and forms—is intended to help *you* develop the best way for you to get ready for a negotiation.

CHAPTER 2

In a Hurry?

Good preparation need not take a lot of time. Clear thinking and a few minutes of focused attention will dramatically improve your effectiveness in negotiation. When you are expecting your negotiations to be short and straightforward, when the stakes do not justify a big investment of time and effort, or even when you would like to take a first step toward a more thorough preparation, we suggest you do a quick sketch of the negotiation terrain. This will leave you better prepared than simply winging it or preparing a list of demands and fallback positions.

For some negotiations, a quick sketch will not be enough, while working through *every* form in this workbook may seem like too much. To prioritize your preparation time for these situations, you should spend a few minutes diagnosing your upcoming negotiation, much as a doctor would check some basic vital signs before proceeding to invest significant time and effort preparing.

One basic premise behind all the work sheets and tools included in this workbook is that having a structure or a system will help you prepare better. Better may not always mean in more detail or taking more time. Better will mean whatever is appropriate for the negotiation. A systematic approach will make you more efficient in those cases where you do not have enough time. It will organize your thinking and clarify what is going on in messy and compli cated situations. It will help you cover all the bases where you might have overlooked something.

In this chapter we introduce two ways to use the seven elements of negotiation described in the introduction as a structured and systematic approach to getting ready to negotiate. With **Sudden Prep,** you will undertake a quick scan of the terrain. This may be all you need for many negotiations. With **Priority Prep**, you will be able to make some informed choices about how to prioritize the time you spend in more in-depth preparation for any particular negotiation.

Sudden prep

The **Sudden Prep** form should help you get a quick feel for what the negotiation is about and where it may go, even if you invest only a few minutes to prepare. Filling out this form is a good way to get started toward a more in-depth preparation, and it may by itself be sufficient for that five-minute telephone negotiation. Spend a few minutes filling out this form, and then keep it handy during your negotiation. It could serve to guide your conversation toward constructive options and reasonable standards for choosing among them.

(This form is intended to provide quick help for an upcoming negotiation.)

SUDDEN PREP

Things I should be ready to put "on the table"

My interests	Options	Legitimacy	Their interests
What I really care about. My wants, needs, concerns, hopes, and fears.	Possible agreements that we might reach.	External standards or precedents that might convince one or both of us that a proposed agreement is fair.	What I think they really care about. Their wants, concerns, hopes, and fears.
1.	1.	1.	1.
2	2.	2.	2.
3	3.	3.	3.
4.	4.	4.	4.
5.	5.	5.	5.

My walk-away alternative

What can I do if I walk away without agreement? Which is the best? What would I really do?

1.

2.

3.

Commitment

If we reach agreement, we commit to some option.

Priority prep

Not every negotiation problem is the same. Some negotiations are between strangers, who know little about each other. Others are between close friends; still others are between individuals who would just as soon not talk to each other, much less try to resolve some outstanding issues between them.

Similarly, not every negotiation poses the same kind of substantive problem. Some negotiations seem to require a simple "yes or no" or "yours or mine" type of answer. Others involve multiple issues, each of which might be resolved in several different ways, leaving the parties with many possible "packages" of solutions to consider.

Not only might there be more than one issue, there may be more than two negotiators. Some of them may be speaking for themselves, and others may be representing clients or constituents.

Beyond these characteristics of negotiations, there are other ways to distinguish among negotiations by what is likely to make them difficult or by what kind of effort is going to be required to make the most of them. For example, some negotiations will require lots of creativity at matching and dovetailing the underlying needs and concerns of the negotiators to create innovative solutions. Others will primarily require injecting some measure of objectivity or legitimacy into what might otherwise be a confrontational discussion.

While all the work sheets and analyses in the subsequent chapters are likely to be useful to the well-prepared negotiator, each bit of preparation takes time, energy, and effort. The reality of life in the modern world is that we cannot always take as much time as we should to do everything we ought to do. To be truly useful, a negotiation preparation guide should help us prioritize our efforts and make good decisions about how to invest our time.

Some of the tools and analysis described in the following chapters are more relevant and useful depending on where you are in the negotiation, what the negotiation is about, and what you know about the other side. While there are no "by the numbers" solutions that can tell you precisely how to prepare for each possible type of negotiation, the diagnostic questions in this section will help you determine where you might invest preparation time most productively.

Your diagnosis might suggest that you should focus on a particular type of preparation. That does not mean that you should stop after you have worked through the tools and work sheets in that chapter. If you have time, work through another chapter or two. In order to be most systematic and productive, you might want to revisit, and perhaps revise, your initial diagnosis after each piece of preparation. Your thinking about the most important challenges may change as you get further into the negotiation.

Consider the following clusters of questions. They represent some typical questions or problems that arise in negotiation. Recognize that not every question within a cluster will be directly applicable; nonetheless, as a place to start, choose the cluster that intrigues you the most. The questions in this cluster define the principal challenges you face in this negotiation. To prepare to overcome these challenges, turn to the chapter indicated by the cluster you have chosen.

What are priority problems to which preparation may be part of the answer?

Interests

Are we likely to be quarreling about our positions, our demands?

Why do I want what I want? Am I sure?

Have I prioritized the issues that are important to me?

Am I confused about "where they are coming from"?

Have I failed to consider what I would want if I were in their shoes?

> If these questions seem central to your negotiation, go to **Chapter 3, Interests,** page 21, and work on those forms.

Options

Does the situation look as though someone must win, the other lose?

Is this a business or family situation where we both have things to gain?

Is it possible that our interests are compatible?

Have we never engaged in joint brainstorming of possibilities?

Have we reached a stalemate?

> If these questions seem central to your negotiation, go to **Chapter 4, Options,** page 33, and work on those forms.

Alternatives

Do I feel I must reach agreement? Do I assume they have to?

Am I uncertain about what I will do if negotiations end without agreement?

Do I feel that they are more powerful? That I am more powerful?

Do I know what they will do if they don't make an agreement?

> If these questions seem central to your negotiation, go to **Chapter 5, Alternatives,** page 45, and work on those forms.

Legitimacy

Am I concerned that I may get ripped off? Am I treated unfairly?

Would it help to give them convincing arguments as to why my proposal is fair for them?

Will I have to explain to others why I agreed to whatever it is we agree on? Will they?

Are there critics who are likely to go after one or both of us?

> If these questions seem central to your negotiation, go to **Chapter 6, Legitimacy,** page 61, and work on those forms.

Communication

Do I know what I want to listen for?

Am I ready to listen actively and empathetically to whatever they say?

Are the messages I want to deliver clear?

Have I thought about how to speak in ways that will make them want to listen?

> If these questions seem central to your negotiation, go to **Chapter 7, Communication,** page 76, and work on those forms.

Relationship

Is our working relationship likely to be difficult?

Am I likely to be defensive or antagonistic with this person?

Could this negotiation damage our relationship?

Might it be difficult for me to talk about money with them?

Is this someone with whom I will need to work in the future?

If these questions seem central to your negotiation, go to **Chapter 8, Relationship,** page 86, and work on those forms.

Commitment

Am I clear on the kind of commitment I can realistically expect at the end of the negotiation?

Am I approaching the time to make a decision?

Is there more to do, after we both say "yes"?

Am I clear on who has authority to make the commitments?

If these questions seem central to your negotiation, go to **Chapter 9, Commitment,** page 96, and work on those forms.

If the matter is important and time is available, you may want to devote some time to each element.

The following examples, developed more fully in chapters 3 through 9, suggest how the previous diagnostic questions can help sort out elements for priority attention.

Some examples

Ken, a produce manager at a supermarket, is up for a promotion as assistant manager for the store. When negotiating his salary, he wants a $5,000 raise. He feels that his salary should be higher for the additional work, and he needs the money. Ken feels that he is stuck in his position and that he may have to make a concession from the $5,000. He thinks that if he "wins," his boss will lose. Ken has ranked the Interests cluster as most important, and the Options cluster as his next priority. Ken should turn to **Chapter 3, Interests,** to help him get out of his "position" and to avoid a battle of "concessions." Ken has looked at only one solution on which he can agree. If time permits, he may also want to turn to **Chapter 4, Options,** to figure out more approaches to the deal for both parties.

Liz, an executive at Wholesale Foods (a national produce distributor), will be negotiating with Terry, a local fruit orchard owner, over this year's terms of agreement: quantities, prices, delivery dates, transportation, etc. She recalls that she and Terry often have different interests and preferences as far as the terms are concerned. She also believes there is the potential of doing more to be mutually profitable. Liz should work on **Chapter 4, Options,** to consider how to create more possibilities and to look at potential trade-offs and gains.

Steve and Cathy are contemplating buying a new car for themselves from a local used-car dealership. They have put together a list of their interests and are ready to get a deal at Your Neighbor Drove It—Used Cars. They are a little worried about the dealer saying "no," and they don't want to feel trapped into accepting something that doesn't fit their needs. Steve and Cathy should start with **Chapter 5, Alternatives,** to think about what they will do if the deal does not satisfy their interests. This chapter will also help them think about what the dealer will do if he thinks their terms are unreasonable. Because they don't want to be ripped off, they might also work on **Chapter 6, Legitimacy,** to determine standards of fairness for the deal.

KidWorld Mfg. Co. and the Assembly Workers of America will be negotiating the health-care aspect of a new three-year contract. This issue has been a problem in the past, with both sides getting stuck in their positions. Both sides want to be able to explain to their constituents why they agreed to a deal. The parties also want a fair deal and do not want to be criticized for whatever decisions they make. **Chapter 6, Legitimacy,** will help the union think about some persuasive standards to bring to the table to help the other side with their decision and to convince their constituents of the fairness of the deal. The union may also want to look at **Chapter 4, Options,** to consider a variety of creative solutions for this issue.

Doris, a two-year tenant, is having trouble with her landlord over some much-needed repairs to her apartment. He has refused to do the work, and she is considering moving. Before starting that hassle, though, she would like to talk to him about the situation. She does not feel listened to and is having trouble understanding his reaction. She thinks he has been rude and unreasonable. Doris should turn to **Chapter 7, Communication,** and **Chapter 8, Relationship,** to think about their individual perspectives of the situation and ways to reframe the discussion so it will go smoother and possibly lead to some solutions.

TrueLab, a designer and manufacturer of laboratory diagnostic equipment, and Advantage Software have been negotiating a possible joint venture to design an expert system that would automate routine work done in labs. Mark, the lead negotiator for TrueLab, has been working with Advantage for six months and would like to complete the negotiations within the next day and a half of meetings. Mark feels it is time to make a decision and that this next meeting will be a crucial one. He also knows there is more to do after both parties say "yes." **Chapter 9, Commitment,** will help Mark consider the product of this crucial meeting and guide him in drafting a table of contents for the agreement of the whole negotiation, illuminating key questions he should consider.

If at this point you have no clear idea of the elements to which you should give priority attention, our suggestion would be to go straight through the next seven chapters, filling out those forms that seem most relevant to your situation.

The Seven Elements of Negotiation

CHAPTER 3

Interests

What Do People Really Want?

All negotiators have interests. These are the needs, desires, and fears that drive our negotiations. Interests are different from positions: those assertions, demands, and offers that parties make during a negotiation. A position is simply one way to satisfy interests. A position is a means, rather than an end. Do you recall the story in *Getting to Yes* about the two children arguing over an orange? One wanted the peel to bake a cake; the other wanted the fruit to make orange juice. Each insisted on a *position*: "Hey, I get the orange!" Eventually they split the difference, dividing the orange in half. But each had underlying *interests* that could have been better met by giving all the fruit to one, all the peel to the other.

To be successful in a negotiation, it is not enough to argue for a position. A negotiated outcome should satisfy the *interests* of both parties, at least better than if there were no agreement. But to satisfy our interests, we need to avoid some common mistakes during preparation.

Common mistakes

Focusing on positions instead of interests

Many people prepare by focusing on positions instead of interests. They figure out an initial demand—what they should ask for—and sometimes a private "bottom line"—the minimum they think acceptable. But there are drawbacks to this approach.

First, it stifles creativity. If a buyer and seller, for example, talk only about their positions on the fee for the transport of goods, they are less likely to discuss a number of other options, such as varying schedules, finding possible loads to ship back so as to save the truck's making an empty trip home, or sharing maintenance responsibilities. By failing to explore the real interests that underlie positions, they, like the children arguing over the orange, are less likely to find mutual gains that could make both sides better off.

Second, preparing only positions may hurt the relationship. If we have thought only about minimum and maximum offers, a negotiation is likely to become a tense contest of wills in which each side feels the need to "stick to their guns" by insisting that their position is correct. Such a battle for dominance strains a relationship.

Thinking only about what we want

We might assume that preparation involves thinking only about what *we* want. Not so. A possible agreement that would meet only our interests is useless if it doesn't also meet the other side's interests well enough so that they are willing to accept it. We must satisfy their interests *at least* acceptably. In addition, by talking exclusively about our own interests, we send a message that we are not willing to work side by side. This makes brainstorming and the search for creative options more difficult.

The well-prepared negotiator

Look for interests behind positions

For each negotiation position that we might take, we should ask ourselves "why?" or "for what purpose?" Why do I want delivery by the fifteenth? For what purpose do I want payment in cash? These questions make us think about the needs that most concern us. They reveal the interests underlying our demands.

If we are unsure about whether something is a position or an interest, we should determine whether there is more than one way to satisfy it. If there is not, as when we say "I demand a company car," it is a position. If so, we should keep probing. In contrast, if there are several ways to satisfy a demand (such as my saying "I want transportation to work" or "I want more status in the company"), it is probably an interest. Even when you have identified an interest, keep probing for more basic underlying interests by asking "why?" and "for what purpose?"

Prioritize your interests

After thinking about our interests, it is useful to prioritize them. This will help us evaluate and compare proposed options more quickly and efficiently. It also may help us achieve the optimal result—we can rework a proposed agreement to address our most important interests. If a deadline is imminent, prioritizing our interests will highlight the issues on which we should spend our time.

Consider the other side's interests

This is a difficult aspect of negotiation. We often expect others to see the world as we do. Yet we need to understand the other side's interests if we want to propose an acceptable option. Once a negotiation is under way, we can inquire about the other side's interests by asking the same questions that we ask ourselves: "why?" and "for what purpose?" We can explore their interests by suggesting proposals and asking "What would be wrong with that?" We might also think hard about why they're saying "no" to a current proposal, and why "no" might make sense from their perspective.

But before a negotiation begins, we should prepare. We might ask them to attend a prenegotiation meeting to discuss interests only. We might call and ask questions, taking care to frame the questions in a way that invites a helpful response: "Am I correct in thinking that you are quite concerned about this issue but not that issue?" "Please help me understand your major concerns." Alternatively, we might consult with people who are in the same profession or industry as our counterpart, or with people in our own organization who hold a similar job. Or we might read articles about them or their business. No matter which approach we use, it will be useful to have some idea of their interests before we go into a negotiation.

The following forms are designed to help you identify and weigh the relevant interests.

INTERESTS 1: *Identify the Relevant Parties*

NEGOTIATOR: _____

COUNTERPART: _____

SUBJECT: _____

Fill in the names of the persons or groups involved in this negotiation. Put yourself as "Negotiator" and the person you are dealing with directly as "Counterpart." In the spaces below, write the names of others who may be significantly affected by the outcome of this negotiation.

People on "my side" who may care about the outcome	People on "their side" who may care about the outcome
Constituents? _____	Constituents? _____
Friends? _____	Friends? _____
Family? _____	Family? _____
Boss? _____	Boss? _____
Others? _____	Others? _____
_____	_____

INTERESTS 2: *Clarify the Interests*

Mine What do I care about?	**Theirs** If I were in their shoes, what would I care or worry about?	**Others** What are the concerns of others who may be significantly affected?
Personal	Personal	Other 1:
		Other 2:
Business	Business	Other 3:

INTERESTS 3: *Probe for Underlying Interests*

NEGOTIATOR: _____

COUNTERPART: _____

SUBJECT: _____

In the left-hand column, list the more important interests for you and your counterpart that you identified on the form **INTERESTS 2.** For each of these, ask yourself "why?" and "for what purpose?" If you discover deeper interests, list them in the second column. Finally, try to rate your own interests by allocating 100 points among them in proportion to their relative importance.

Important interests (from **INTERESTS 2**)	Basic or underlying interests (Ask yourself "why?" and "for what purpose?")	Relative importance (Allocate 100 points)
Mine		
Theirs		

An example

Ken is the produce manager at "Saneway," a large supermarket that is part of a national chain. After completing a few management courses offered by his employer, as well as five years of service at the supermarket, he is up for a promotion to assistant manager. He is about to negotiate his new salary and the terms of his new position.

Ken wants to be promoted to the assistant manager position because it pays more and requires a greater variety of responsibilities. He wants a raise of at least five thousand dollars because: (1) he needs the money; (2) he thinks the job requires more work, responsibility, and headaches, so it should pay more; (3) he's heard a rumor that Wayne, who held this position before relocating to another store, was paid five thousand dollars more than Ken's current salary; and (4) he thinks he deserves it.

Ken is twenty-eight years old and has a bachelor's degree in English literature. He has always had an interest in going back to school and getting a master's degree (although he's not sure what subject to pursue). Money has been an obstacle to a graduate-level education. His only source of funds is what he makes at Saneway, and he really doesn't want and can't afford to take out any more loans. Ken lives in a modest but comfortable studio apartment with his fat cat, Margo. The apartment is at least forty-five minutes away by car from the Saneway store where he is currently working, and there is no easily accessible public transportation. He has recently traded in his beat-up Volkswagen bug for a new Toyota pickup truck.

INTERESTS 1: *Identify the Relevant Parties*

NEGOTIATOR: Ken
COUNTERPART: Lou
SUBJECT: Promotion

Fill in the names of the persons or groups involved in this negotiation. Put yourself as "Negotiator" and the person you are dealing with directly as "Counterpart." In the spaces below, write the names of others who may be significantly affected by the outcome of this negotiation.

People on "my side" who may care about the outcome	**People on "their side" who may care about the outcome**
Constituents? _____	Constituents? Consumers
Friends? Jessie, my significant other	Friends? Colleagues at work
Family? _____	Family? _____
Boss? _____	Boss? Regional director
Others? Margo, my cat	Others? Vendors
_____	Saneway Corporation

DATE PREPARED: _____

INTERESTS 2: *Clarify the Interests*

NEGOTIATOR: Ken

COUNTERPART: Lou

SUBJECT: Promotion

Mine What do I care about?	**Theirs** If I were in their shoes, what would I care or worry about?	**Others** What are some of the concerns of others who may be significantly affected?
Personal Short-term 1. ~~$5000~~ not get taken 2. enough money for rent, cat food and care, car payments, etc. 3. vacation days 4. health care Long-term 1. opportunity to grow and advance 2. go back to school	**Personal** 1. I look good 2. Be perceived as fair	**Other 1:** Other employees -a good, fair, and consistent manager -good working relationship -don't want Ken to get more than he deserves **Other 2:** Consumers -cheapest prices -fresh produce -quality food -fast & friendly service -store looks nice & clean

Business
 Short-term
 1. promoted to assistant store manager
 2. respect from employer, colleagues, and subordinates
 3. setting a good precedent
 4. incentives and bonuses
 	
 Long-term
 1. maybe get transferred to closer store
 2. be promoted to manager
	Business
	 Short-term
	 1. pay lowest salary (what he really cares about is profit)
	 2. need someone flexible/able to adapt to changing environment/policies
	 3. satisfy customers
	 4. assistant store manager needs to:
	   a) make accurate sales projections & salary predictions
	   b) write memos to district managers & department heads
	
	 Long-term
	 1. relationship with vendors
	 2. profit
	 3. precedent
	 4. groom a loyal & committed employee
		Other 3:
		 Vendors
		 -long-term relationship
		 -access to display space
		 -sell as much as possible at highest price
		 -steady market stream

INTERESTS 3: *Probe for Underlying Interests*

NEGOTIATOR: Ken
COUNTERPART: Lou
SUBJECT: Promotion

In the left-hand column, list the more important interests for you and your counterpart that you identified on the **INTERESTS 2** form. For each of these, ask yourself "why?" and "for what purpose?" If you discover deeper interests, list them in the second column. Finally, try to rate your own interests by allocating 100 points among them in proportion to their relative importance.

Important interests (from **INTERESTS 2**)	Basic or underlying interests (Ask yourself "why?" and "for what purpose?")	Relative importance (Allocate 100 points)
Mine		
Money for living expenses	1. Food, lodging, cat care	30
	2. Fair compensation	10
Promotion to asst. manager	3. Better status	10
	4. Challenge & growth	20
Future opportunities to advance	5. Feel I'm not at a "dead end"	20
Benefits (vacation, health care, etc.)	6. Peace of mind	5
	7. Feel well treated	5
Theirs		
Pay lowest salary possible	1. Profitable store	
Good assistant manager	2. Someone to delegate to	
	3. Accurate sales projections	
	4. Someone to take care of writing memos to headquarters	
	5. Someone flexible	
Happy customers	6. Continued sales	
	7. Good reputation	

Preparing for the salary negotiation with Lou, Ken obviously needs to think about what he wants. He has started to fill in some preparation forms for his upcoming meeting.

Ken has begun his preparation by identifying some of the people involved in this transaction. We want to be clear about with whom we are negotiating. Who is the individual we will be facing? What organizations are involved? Who are the people who aren't at the negotiation table but who may still be interested or affected by this deal? As shown on the first form, **INTERESTS 1:** *Identify the Relevant Parties,* Ken and Lou, his boss, are the primary players in this negotiation, but there are others who may be interested in or affected by their transaction. Saneway definitely has a stake in this negotiation. Colleagues, consumers, and vendors may be interested, as well as Ken's cat and significant other.

On the second form, **INTERESTS 2:** *Clarify the Interests,* Ken has started listing some of his short- and long-term personal and business interests. Ken's first impulse was to write "$5,000" at the top of the form. He then crossed it out because he thought that maybe "$5,000" sounded more like a position than an interest. When he thought further about *why* he wanted $5,000, he realized it was really because he wanted to be treated fairly. Ken wanted to be paid no less than Wayne, the previous assistant manager, was paid. He believed that he was at least as qualified as Wayne. He also thought that what he really cared about was having enough money to pay his basic living costs and car payments. Of course, he would also like extra money just to spend on personal things.

He went on to list some of his other interests, including short- and long-term business interests. He wasn't quite sure whether some of them were positions or interests, but he tried his best to list interests.

Ken also thought about Lou's interests. Lou's interests need to be satisfied so that Lou will be able to say "yes" to a deal. This part was particularly difficult for Ken. Although he knows and likes Lou pretty well, he had to push hard to try to step into Lou's shoes to generate some of the items on the list (especially the personal ones). Because Ken doesn't know all the constraints Lou faces, he could make only his best guess at Lou's key interests.

Finally, Ken took into account the interests of third parties who may be affected by this negotiation. These third-party interests will need to be satisfied at least tolerably, because they are affected and they may affect the negotiators. He and Lou might reach a great deal, but it could be so controversial or so against the interests of others that the deal would never be realized because of their opposition. Ken's significant other, cat, colleagues, various departments of his supermarket, the national headquarters of the supermarket, the U.S. government, food growers, vendors, and consumers are all to some extent interested parties, but some of these are more likely than others to have an impact on the negotiation.

After he filled out the **INTERESTS 2** form, Ken probed further, for the more basic or fundamental reasons behind his interests. He also speculated a bit about what Lou might *really* care about. The form **INTERESTS 3:** *Probe for Underlying Interests* helped Ken to dig a little deeper and then prioritize his interests by allocating one hundred points among his listed interests.

Allocating points is difficult, and there are no clear right and wrong answers. Attempting to do so, however, is important because it helps us consider trade-offs among various interests. For example, it is not as critical for Ken to satisfy the interest of improving his status at the store as it is to have the opportunity to grow and advance. Nor is the number of vacation days as important as enough money for rent and other payments. In this way, Ken is able to focus on his higher-priority interests.

CHAPTER 4

Options

What Are Possible Agreements or Bits of an Agreement?

Out of diversity—of perspectives, resources, or interests—comes the opportunity to create value. Negotiation is not about papering over differences or persuading others to want what we want. It is about recognizing how those differences can help make each of us better off than we would have been without a deal.

In **Chapter 3: Interests** we considered interests—the wants, needs, fears, and concerns—of negotiators and those whom they represent. Those interests are the building blocks of a possible agreement. Options, on the other hand, are possible solutions to a negotiation—ways to fit those building blocks (sometimes shaped a bit like pieces of a jigsaw puzzle) together to satisfy the negotiators and create value.

The best negotiations are those in which a number of possible options have been explored. Just because a particular resolution is the first that occurred to one of you, and the first that you could both accept, does not mean it is the best one. The more options that are generated, the greater the chance that one of them will effectively reconcile the differing interests of the parties. To achieve an agreement on such an option, it helps to go in well prepared.

Common mistakes

Taking a narrow, one-sided focus

Often negotiators prepare for a negotiation by trying to figure out what they want, and perhaps by going so far as to outline as many as three variations on the theme: what they would love to get; the least they would settle for; and some "realistic" point in between. In doing so, negotiators prepare only to haggle to and fro along some arbitrary range. Knowing one fantasy aspiration tells them only what to ask for, not what a variety of possible solutions might be. Establishing a "bottom line" may serve as a signal that at some point they should walk out in a huff. It does not provide a good sense of what they might do after they walk out. And accepting as a realistic goal some midpoint between fantasy and bottom line will dampen their expectations and, in all likelihood, limit the value they will obtain in the negotiation.

If you prepare by establishing arbitrary positions along a continuum, you will tend to make two cardinal mistakes of preparation, both of which may lead to adversarial, positional negotiations.

1. A focus on what you want, without regard for the interests of the other side, will leave you unprepared to respond constructively to their ideas and concerns.
2. A single position, even with some fallbacks, will leave you unprepared to engage in real problem-solving with the other side or to consider a broad and rich universe of possible solutions.

Neglecting the value in differences

Many negotiators tend to approach a negotiation as an exercise in "resolving differences" or "reaching consensus." Although dealing well with differences is an important part of managing working relationships, if you prepare to minimize differences or acquiesce for the sake of the relationship, you are preparing to leave value on the table. It leads to "least common denominator" solutions, rather than the real benefit that negotiation can create. The well-prepared negotiator is aware of the differences and has considered how they might be put to work to create more value for both parties.

The well-prepared negotiator

Often, just by looking at a list of each side's interests, we can identify some possible ways to satisfy those interests. Preparing a list of such possibilities in advance of a negotiation takes you two steps further than the typical "I know what I want and I know what I will settle for" style of preparation. Such options both take into account the interests of the other negotiator and are more varied and creative than simple bargaining positions. The tools and suggestions in **Chapter 3: Interests** are designed to help you understand the interests of the parties. In this chapter we try to go one step further—to help you prepare to create more value for each negotiator. Classifying the interests by how important they are to each of you serves as a guide for how to proceed to expand the pie before dividing it.

Look for ways to work together to make more

Negotiators often quarrel over interests that are of high importance to both. This reflects the common, often-reinforced assumption that if we both value it, then the only thing left to do is divide it up between us, in an adversarial, zero-sum way: more for you means less for me. This assumption ignores the power of working together to expand the pie. If two negotiators both want something, the first question that comes to mind should not be "How can I get the bigger share?" but "How might we make more?"

With an eye on the real purpose of negotiation—satisfying the interests of the parties—it is instructive to look at the skills and resources you each have and look for ways to combine them or collaborate in their application to enhance the value each will receive. In particular, consider the following ways to create value:

- With similar skills and resources, the parties can work together to achieve economies of scale. It may be cheaper for one of you to produce enough for two, than for you each to produce enough for one. Or perhaps by combining purchasing power, you can get a better discount than each of you could separately. That is value that is now going somewhere else (perhaps even up in smoke), and which by collaborating, you can put on the table.

- With different skills and resources, you may be able to work together to create what neither of you could do on your own. What better example do we need than two toddlers at the beach, one of whom has a bucket and the other a shovel? Together, there is nothing they can't build.

- Regardless of whether your resources are the same or different, consider options for joint benefit, as opposed to separate or independent benefit. There are some pies you can make that do not later require splitting, because you can both enjoy them together. For example, a donation to a jointly chosen charity allows you both to benefit without having to divvy something up. Similarly, a jointly sponsored conference that benefits both of you in public relations, network, educational opportunities, etc., allows you both to create something you can each benefit from without diminishing it for the other. One agreement can enhance the reputation of both.

Find value in differences

Differences fuel the engines of commerce. Without different perceptions of the value of a share of stock, there would be no active stock market; no one would be willing to buy a share for more than the seller thought it was worth. Without different preferences over which team to root for, sporting events would be a bore. In negotiation, as in life, it takes two to tango, and if one likes to lead while the other prefers to follow, they will have a much better time.

In a negotiation, anything that you value highly and the other negotiator does not (or vice versa) represents an opportunity to create value. To recognize that value and to turn it from potential value to real value often requires hard work. But the very exercise of looking for possible trade-offs that confer significant value on one side, at little or no cost to the other, is likely to leave you substantially better prepared to take the matter up and turn at least some of that potential into reality. Consider the following common sources of difference:

Risk   Some people hate it; others adore it. Often large institutions are better equipped to handle it than individuals. Look for differences in risk aversion between the negotiators and consider whether one side could more easily (or less expensively) bear or insure against a risk than the other.

Timing   People work on different clocks. Some place a lot of value on proceeding slowly and deliberately, taking time to plan each step of the way. Others are always seemingly in a hurry and thrive on the fast pace at which they lead their activities. Look for the possibility that what is impossible this month is easy next month, or what is unaffordable under next year's budget can be scraped out of unused discretionary funds this year.

Perceptions   For some, "what other people will think" is more relevant than what actually happened; for others, the opinions of third parties are the unwanted interventions of busybodies, to be studiously ignored. Look for ways that one side can have a public victory if it needs it, while the other receives something in currencies it values more.

Marginal value of the same item   Many people find that when they have several of something, they value the last one somewhat less than those that came before. To borrow a classic example from economics textbooks, if I already have three bananas, I am less likely to value a fourth one as highly as I might value an orange, of which I have only one. If you, on the other hand, have five oranges and no bananas, we may both be better off by trading some of our fruit. Differences in the marginal value to each party of some of the goods under negotiation can thus create opportunities to improve the overall value they each receive.

None of these value-creating trade-offs is guaranteed to work, however. Easy-to-follow recipes for success in negotiation do not exist. Good options can often be invented jointly during a negotiation. But advance preparation and the systematic consideration of opportunities to create value will enable you to identify the possibilities, think about them ahead of time, and take some initiative in trying to create value instead of just quarreling over it. The following forms should help.

OPTIONS 1: *Create Options to Meet Interests*

NEGOTIATOR: _____

COUNTERPART: _____

SUBJECT: _____

Look at your **INTERESTS 3** form, then list possible ways to meet the interests on both sides. (List interests in order of their relative importance.)

My interests	Possible options	Their interests

OPTIONS 2: *Find Ways to Maximize Joint Gains*

Consider ways to combine skills and resources to satisfy key interests on both sides.

	Inventory of skills and resources	Combine similar resources to produce value	Combine different resources to produce value
Me			
Them			

An example

Liz is a regional manager with Wholesale Foods, a large and growing national produce distributor. She is responsible for managing relationships with suppliers, mostly small farmers in the state, as well as customers of Wholesale Foods, who range from small corner grocers to the stores of the largest regional supermarket chain. One of the suppliers with whom she must negotiate is Terry, the owner of a small fruit orchard in the northeast corner of the state.

As the manager of a large territory, Liz has to worry about her profitability, which in turn is a function of the price at which she buys and sells produce. But her profitability is also affected by the amount of effort it takes her to get the produce to market and how much she has to spend to overcome glitches in her delivery system. For example, if a farmer is late with his deliveries, Liz has to spend money to get produce from somewhere else, usually at a higher price, to meet her obligations to her customers; or if a farmer delivers fruit in bulk, Liz has to spend money to crate it properly. Similarly, her profitability is related to the price she can get for the produce from her customers. If she can develop a reputation for being a source of "quality" produce, she can get an extra few cents per pound over average market prices, which rapidly adds up to big profits. To manage some of these risks, Liz maintains a small fleet of closed-bed trucks capable of traveling around the state and employs a few more workers than are absolutely necessary in her warehouses.

Terry is his own boss, running a farm that has been in his family for three generations. Over his lifetime he has seen the farm experiment with a number of different crops, but at significant risk: a bad harvest with a supposedly improved strain of one of his traditional crops could wipe him out. Similarly, the risk of planting something different and not being able to sell it at a good price could mean not being able to pay off the season's debts at harvest time, which in turn would mean not being able to buy needed stocks and supplies at planting time. Terry has one open-bed pickup truck he uses to bring in supplies and deliver fruit. He hires only seasonal help, at planting and harvest times.

Each year, Liz and Terry get together and discuss terms: quantities and prices for his fruit, the dates on which delivery should be made, how the fruit will be crated, etc. Although they get along, Liz has the sense that there is more they could do that would be mutually profitable.

OPTIONS 1: *Create Options to Meet Interests*

Look at your **INTERESTS 3** form, then list possible ways to meet the interests on both sides. (List interests in order of their relative importance.)

My interests	Possible options	Their interests
1. Revenue	Pay premium price for premium quality	1. Revenue
2. Quality	Pay bonus for on-time delivery	2. Quality
3. Reliability	Share cost of crating	3. Reliability
4. Crating	Advance cash at planting time, to risk on new products	4. Crating
5. Competitive advantage over other wholesalers	Exclusive deal in exchange for guaranteed contract to buy all that Terry produces that meets minimum quality standards	5. Quick and effective harvest
6. Access to other products		6. Liquidity during planting
7. Brand image		7. Shipping insurance

OPTIONS 2: *Find Ways to Maximize Joint Gains*

Consider ways to combine skills and resources to satisfy key interests on both sides.

	Inventory of skills and resources	Combine similar resources to produce value	Combine different resources to produce value
Me	Money Closed-bed trucks Steady labor Customers Market savvy	1. We might pool our trucks and use each for what it's best suited. 2. We might pool our purchases to get a better price (fuel, tires, spare parts).	1. I could provide extra labor at harvest time to help pack produce in smaller crates. 2. We could work together to identify specialty produce he could grow and I could finance and market. 3. We could put labels on the best fruit to create a positive brand image. 4. I could advance Terry some payment at planting time.
Them	Produce Land Seasonal labor Farming experience Open-bed truck Opportunity to recognize and separate the "best" fruit		

Using **OPTIONS 1:** *Create Options to Meet Interests,* Liz has developed some ideas for possible pieces of a deal. At the top of both lists, we can see those things that Liz expects are important to both of them, if only because she knows that they have expressed interests about them in prior negotiations. These are revenue (how much will Liz pay out and how much will Terry receive for a season's harvest); what quality produce will Terry provide Liz; reliability (of Terry's supply to Liz, and of Liz as a customer for Terry); and what type of crating, if any, will be used (Terry tends to prefer to deliver his fruit in bulk, filling his open-bed truck as fast as possible at harvest time, in order to get each load delivered and the truck back to the farm to pick up more. Liz prefers to receive fruit already packed into the fifty-pound crates she uses for wholesale distribution; these crates also stack better in her warehouses, while waiting to be delivered). Collectively, these are the things about which she and Terry typically bargain.

After the first few items in the "My Interests" column, Liz has noted some additional interests she has, which she expects Terry does not share or even think much about. These have not generally been subjects of negotiation; they are just of interest to Liz. Similarly, moving down the "Their Interests" column, Liz has noted some things she assumes are important to Terry, from what she knows about farmers in general and him in particular. Terry is not one to share a lot of information about things he considers to be "his business," so Liz's preparation in this regard is mostly educated guesswork.

In the center column, Liz has listed some possible options to satisfy each of their interests. These will take further work to make them more precise, but they suggest some avenues to explore with Terry.

In **OPTIONS 2:** *Find Ways to Maximize Joint Gains,* Liz has tried to stretch her thinking and look for previously unexplored opportunities. Liz has identified some skills and resources she and Terry each have. By working with these, she considers how she and Terry might cooperate to create more value for each of them, with respect to those interests she listed at the top of both columns in **OPTIONS 1:** *Create Options to Meet Interests*—the things that they both value highly and traditionally have spent most of their energy bargaining over. While her responses in these boxes will not eliminate the need to negotiate constructively over such things as price and quality standards, they do suggest some other avenues to explore with Terry to help each of them satisfy their interests more effectively.

For example, Liz and Terry might consider whether and how to pool their different trucks, to use each for what it is best suited—Terry might count on Liz's closed-bed trucks to haul his produce from the northeast corner of the state to the Wholesale Foods warehouses more rapidly at harvest time, and Liz might call on Terry's open-bed truck to make some deliveries of odd-sized or bulk goods to some of her customers. Or Liz could send some of her spare warehouse staff to Terry's farm at harvest time, to help him pack the fruit into the kinds of crates that Wholesale Foods prefers, saving both of them time and money over current practice. In order to meet both of their interests in increased overall revenue, they might collaborate to identify specialty or gourmet products that Terry could grow on small parcels, under Wholesale Foods contracts. Such an option would also give Liz the more diversified product offerings and competitive advantage she seeks and Terry the year-round liquidity he would like, without the risk that such an effort might otherwise entail.

This kind of preparation does not guarantee success in a negotiation. It may well be that after further, joint consideration, none of these options will prove to be practical. But by exploring them, Liz and Terry will be starting down a path of looking to put more value on the table before thinking about how to divide it up, instead of bargaining over who has to win and who has to lose on issues like price and crating.

CHAPTER 5

Alternatives

What Will I Do If We Do Not Agree?

Not every negotiation concludes with an agreement. Nor should it. There are times when you can do better by walking away, because the costs of the proposed agreement exceed its benefits or because someone else is in a position to offer you a better deal.

Alternatives, as the name suggests, are other ways of accomplishing something. In negotiation, that something is satisfying your interests. Your interests can be satisfied in two different ways: through a negotiated solution—that is, an option, using the vocabulary of this workbook—or through some kind of self-help alternative—that is, some action you take independently or an arrangement you make with someone other than the person with whom you are negotiating. In every negotiation, if you stop to think about it, you will be able to come up with several possible alternatives (not all of them may be attractive, but it is important to know that they exist). The best of these is what we call your BATNA—your **B**est **A**lternative **T**o a **N**egotiated **A**greement. For the outcome of a negotiation to be truly considered a success, you should come up with an option that is better for you than your BATNA, or you should walk away.

Preparing your BATNA before the negotiation is absolutely essential to helping you decide when to walk or when to stay and talk. Many negotiators come up with a "bottom line" before they start a negotiation—but if that bottom line is a number you have pulled out of the air, it does not really help you make decisions. If you get pushed to your bottom line, should you walk away? You should do so only if your bottom line is based on what you could get elsewhere, your alternatives; and only if the best of those, your BATNA, is better than what is on the table. Otherwise, how do you know your "bottom line" was realistic? Moreover, how do you know that you can do better outside the negotiation than in it? If you know your BATNA, and it is better than what your counterpart is offering, you can head for the door with confidence. If it is not, you know it is time to get very creative at the negotiation table, and that you are not being weak by failing to walk out in a huff.

Common mistakes

Not thinking of a BATNA

Negotiators make two common preparation mistakes regarding their BATNA. Some negotiators walk into a negotiation without knowing what they will do if they cannot reach agreement. That tends to make them insecure and unsure of when they should keep negotiating and when they should start heading for the door. Just think of a time when you were in a similar situation: someone said, "This is it," and you either had to give in or call their bluff (and risk it may not be one!). Without knowing what your BATNA is, a whole negotiation may come down to bluster and a roll of the dice.

Assuming BATNA is the "same old thing"

The other common mistake is to assume you know your BATNA, without first thinking more creatively about other ways to satisfy your interests. In labor negotiations, for example, unions have traditionally viewed the strike as their BATNA. Even though striking is sometimes the only way to convince management to accept their demands, that may not be the union's only way to accomplish what they want. Under some circumstances, other alternatives may be more effective, less costly, or both. For example, certain lobbying or public relations efforts may pay off, work-to-rule or job-slowdowns may send the necessary message without incurring risks of a full-blown strike, negotiating with a potential acquirer may satisfy some economic and human relations interests, etc.

The well-prepared negotiator

Know your BATNA

Never underestimate the power of knowing what you will do if you do not reach agreement. It will give you much greater confidence during the negotiation, whether you reach agreement or not. It will keep you from making mistakes by accepting something that is not good enough—compared not to some arbitrary notion of what you or others want, or think you can get, but to something concrete and feasible. It will help you decide when to walk away and when to stay, without all the anxiety that such a decision tends to provoke. Investing time to think about not just one alternative, but several ways to satisfy your interests, and determining which alternative is best will pay off, even when you never have to use your BATNA. Remember that your BATNA is not just another way to pressure them to give in. It is a powerful concept to help you focus on what you really want to accomplish, and the different ways in which you can do so, without having to accept a deal with terms that do not well satisfy your interests.

Strengthen your BATNA

Alternatives are rarely fixed in stone. Taking a moment to step back and think about how to make your BATNA easier, more probable, or better at satisfying your interests can improve the outcome of many of your negotiations. Think about it. If you will only accept a deal that is better than your BATNA, by improving your BATNA you guarantee yourself a better result: if you reach an agreement, it will be better and if you do not, your BATNA will be better too. Having a strong BATNA, and knowing so, will also boost your confidence during the negotiation.

Consider their BATNA

All negotiators have a BATNA, whether they have thought about it or not. As you prepare to negotiate with someone, it would be useful to know at what point they should walk out of the negotiation. While you may never be able to figure out such a subjective thing with any degree of confidence, you may be able to make a pretty good guess at what they might do if you do not reach agreement. And if you can do that, you can think about how to make the choice less attractive to them—whether by making their BATNA harder to implement or less valuable, or just by affecting their perception of how unwise or costly such an alternative might be.

The following forms should help you develop your BATNA and estimate theirs.

ALTERNATIVES 1: *Think of My Alternatives to a Negotiated Agreement*

My key interests:

What could I do to satisfy my interests if we do not reach an agreement?

Possible alternatives	Pros	Cons

Of my alternatives, what will I really do if no agreement is reached (my BATNA)? Why?

What can I do to improve my BATNA? (Write down concrete steps you could take to improve your BATNA even before you go into the negotiation.)

ALTERNATIVES 3: *Identify Alternatives Open to the Other Side*

NEGOTIATOR: _____
COUNTERPART: _____
SUBJECT: _____

Their key interests:

What could they do to satisfy their interests if we do not reach an agreement?

Alternatives	Pros	Cons

ALTERNATIVES 4: *Estimate Their BATNA*

What would I do in their shoes? (Which of their self-help alternatives looks best for them?)

How might I legitimately make their BATNA less attractive?

By making it harder to pursue?	By influencing their perception of how unwise or costly it might be?

An example

Steve and Cathy are thinking of buying a new car. They have looked around a bit at cars their friends and neighbors are driving and have checked the local paper for advertisements. They think they will want to trade in their current jalopy, a twelve-year-old gas guzzler with over 100,000 miles.

Steve and Cathy have done some advance preparation, thinking hard about their interests in this transaction. They care a lot about the car's gas mileage, both because of the cost and because they worry about the environmental damage that burning fuel causes. Steve and Cathy are expecting to have a child sometime in the next couple of years, and they would like a practical and safe car in which they could put the legally required infant restraints when the time comes. Because they commute to work together (Cathy drops Steve off and parks at an uncovered lot near her office) and use that time to chat, they don't much care about the car's sound system, but they do care about the car's appearance and its ability to stand up to the weather year-round. Finally, being relatively ignorant about automotive mechanics, they would prefer a car that would not give them much trouble and a reliable, convenient service center to take it to when necessary. The dealership closest to their home, and therefore the most convenient, is called Your Neighbor Drove It—Used Cars.

ALTERNATIVES 1: *Think of My Alternatives to a Negotiated Agreement*

My key interests:

1. Good gas mileage
2. Safety (infant seats)
3. Looks
4. Reliability
5. Convenient service

What could I do to satisfy my interests if we do not reach an agreement?

Possible alternatives	Pros	Cons
1. Buy from classified ad	Cheaper	No service or reliability guarantee; have to sell jalopy same way; less convenient; not a good selection
2. Buy new	More reliable; warranted; built-in infant seat option; new paint, etc.	More expensive
3. Commute on public transportation	Better for the environment; cheaper	Less convenient (different buses: one unreliable; other fine)
4. Another dealership	May get better deal if promise referrals	Farther away; don't know anyone who's shopped there

Of my alternatives, what will I really do if no agreement is reached (my BATNA)? Why?

#4: Another dealership—meets most of the same interests as buying from Your Neighbor Drove It, except convenience of location.

What can I do to improve my BATNA? (Write down concrete steps you could take to improve your BATNA even before you go into the negotiation.)

1) Call Better Business Bureau and ask for references;
2) Find out if local mechanic could come with us, in exchange for promise to bring car to him for service;
3) Visit the other dealership to see what they have.

ALTERNATIVES 3: *Identify Alternatives Open to the Other Side*

Their key interests:

1. Commissions
2. Referrals
3. Service business
4. Look good to boss

What could they do to satisfy their interests if we do not reach an agreement?

Alternatives	Pros	Cons
1. Sell to another customer	Uncertain; may or may not get better price	Have to wait; may have to advertise
2. Sell to Rent-A-Bargain	Fast and easy	Get less money; if it turns out to be a lemon, will hurt future business with them
3. Sell to another dealer	Relatively easy—just make a few calls	Less money; looks bad for our business

ALTERNATIVES 4: *Estimate Their BATNA*

What would I do in their shoes? (Which of their self-help alternatives looks best for them?)

I'd find out how much I could sell it to Rent-A-Bargain for, but keep trying to sell to another customer.

How might I legitimately make their BATNA less attractive?

By making it harder to pursue ?	By influencing their perception of how unwise or costly it might be?
Leave an offer with a small deposit good for one week and let his boss know. (If he knows it is "sold," he's less likely to put effort or publicity into improving the offer.)	Find out what Rent-A-Bargain might pay for a similar car. Comment on number of similar cars advertised in the paper.

Before Steve and Cathy went to their local used-car dealership, Your Neighbor Drove It—Used Cars, they spent a few minutes thinking about their BATNA—what they think their best walk-away alternative might be. That way, if the salesperson at Your Neighbor Drove It tried to pressure them into a decision, they would know what kind of prospective deal they should continue to discuss, and what kind of deal they should walk away from. Take a look at how they filled out form **ALTERNATIVES 1:** *Think of My Alternatives to a Negotiated Agreement.*

As you can see, Steve and Cathy have identified 5 key interests that they will use to measure how good each alternative is. In no particular order, they have identified: (1) good gas mileage; (2) safety (infant seats); (3) looks; (4) reliability; and (5) convenient service. Interestingly, they did not list "price" or getting rid of their jalopy as key interests. (It is worth noting that we sometimes forget the obvious.) Being a bit more systematic is always better preparation for a negotiation. If you find yourself unsure of what your interests are in a particular negotiation, you should take a look at the forms and advice in **Chapter 3, Interests.**

Steve and Cathy have identified four possible alternatives: (1) buying a car through the classified ads; (2) buying a new car; (3) commuting to work on public transportation (and keeping the jalopy for weekends); and (4) going to a different used-car dealer, one township away. As they analyzed each one, they noted some of the benefits and drawbacks of each alternative relative to their interests. Here's where they first noticed that they had omitted some things that were important to them from the list of interests. As you can see, they noted the relative cost of some of the alternatives, and the likelihood they'd be able to sell the jalopy.

Steve and Cathy used this information and form **ALTERNATIVE 2:** *Select and Improve My BATNA* to consider what they'll do if no agreement is reached. In some cases, it will be relatively obvious from among the alternatives which is your BATNA. In others, you will need to do some more homework to be able to evaluate them. Here, for example, it helps that Steve and Cathy have already looked in their local paper and have a sense of how well the selection of cars offered for sale might meet their interests (not very well). They also know that public transportation, although a possibility, is not terribly convenient. The bus that goes to Cathy's office is not very reliable and is often quite crowded. The one that goes in Steve's direction is better, but stops several blocks away from his store. Furthermore, by taking different buses, they would lose the opportunity to talk on the way to work every morning and evening.

This helps them decide that their BATNA is probably to buy a car from a different dealership—most likely a used-car lot in a neighboring town.

If they think that is their BATNA, they should think about how to improve it. After all, Steve and Cathy will only accept a deal from Your Neighbor Drove It that is at least as good as that they can get from the dealership in the next town. Knowing this, they are more certain about what kind of deal they can get at the new dealership. The better this alternative deal meets their interests, the more confident they will feel in negotiating with the salesperson at Your Neighbor Drove It. In order to improve their BATNA, Steve and Cathy will make some phone calls and then take a drive out to the other dealership to check out models and prices before they do any serious negotiating at Your Neighbor Drove It.

You should consider a number of possible alternatives, evaluate them, and think about how to make them real. Even though there may be one alternative that seems obvious, don't stop there. Think about three or four different ways—outside your current negotiation—to satisfy your interests. Then think about how well each one meets your interests and about what you would do if you wanted to pursue that alternative instead of accepting an offer in the negotiation. Choose the alternative that best meets your key interests. This is your BATNA. Can you improve it? The better your BATNA, the more confident you will feel in the negotiation, because you know you will not have to accept an offer that is not at least as good for you as your BATNA.

Whether they call it that or not, the person with whom you are negotiating also has a BATNA. They will do a deal with you only if what you offer is better than their walk-away alternative.

Steve and Cathy tried to get into the shoes of the salesperson from Your Neighbor Drove It (as much as they might be able to do without actually meeting him) and invested a bit of time in thinking about what some of his alternatives might be. They filled out form **ALTERNATIVES 3:** *Identify Alternatives Open to the Other Side.*

They started, of course, by thinking about his possible interests and came up with four likely ones: (1) earn commissions from sales; (2) get referral business; (3) generate future business for service department; and (4) look good to his boss.

Based on those interests, it seemed to them that the salesperson's most likely alternatives would be: (1) to try to sell the same car to a different customer; (2) to try to sell the car to a nearby car-rental outfit that specializes in older, used cars (Rent-A-Bargain); or (3) to sell the car to another dealer or a wholesaler.

Each of those alternatives meets the salesperson's interests to some extent, some more so than others. For example, continuing to try to sell the car on the lot might bring in more money, but it may cost more in advertising and carrying costs and is an uncertain bet. Selling the car—either to the rental place or another dealer—may mean substantially less money, and to some extent may mean admitting that he cannot sell it himself within a reasonable period of time.

A final piece of Steve and Cathy's preparation on the question of the salesperson's BATNA is to consider whether they can make his BATNA even less attractive (and their offer more so, by comparison). Form **ALTERNATIVES 4: *Estimate Their BATNA*** helped with this task. Without knowing more than they currently do, it may be hard for them to evaluate those alternatives very well, but with a couple of phone calls, they might learn enough to be able to counter the salesperson's boasts of how good his alternatives might be. For example, Rent-A-Bargain may tell them how much they might pay for a similar car, or their bank (which probably finances used-cars lots) may tell them about how much the wholesale value of the car might be, based on industry norms. By being a bit assertive—and leaving a small deposit to guarantee their offer for a week—they may also make it less likely that the salesperson (or his boss) will want to spend much energy to pursue the alternative of looking for another customer for that particular car.

CHAPTER 6

Legitimacy

What Criteria Will I Use
to Persuade Each of Us That We Are Not
Being Ripped Off?

However well we understand the interests of the other side and however ingeniously we invent ways of reconciling interests, we will almost always face the harsh reality of interests that conflict. Some negotiators try to resolve these issues on the basis of willpower: "I am more stubborn than you are, so give me what I want!" or "I demand fifty dollars, and that's that." But effective negotiators *persuade* their counterparts. They understand that it is usually more persuasive to convince the other side that a given result would be *fair* rather than to convince by stubbornness. Arguing about what they will or won't do creates a contest in which the other side knows that stubbornness will be rewarded. That is not an incentive we would like to create for either side. We would like both parties to be open to new ideas.

We are not saying "Be fair to be nice," or even "Be fair to produce a fair agreement." Those are possible by-products. We are suggesting that criteria of fairness are valuable as a sword to persuade others and as a shield to protect ourselves from being unfairly treated.

To protect me from being ripped off, I would like to know that a proposed outcome is fair as measured by some external standard. And to convince the other side that they are not being ripped off, I would like to persuade them that what I am asking them to do is legitimate—it is the right thing to do. If I am going to persuade myself and the other side that a given agreement is fair, I will want to have on hand some external standards, precedents, or other objective criteria of legitimacy. Such principles and standards help negotiators choose among the options they have generated and give both sides something to point to when explaining why they accepted a negotiated agreement.

Preparing to persuade requires thinking about, even researching, those things that will enable you to show your counterpart that he or she should agree: that the agreement makes sense and that they can explain the agreement to others. Such a result requires thinking hard about standards or opinions they would find persuasive and how to bring those to bear on your negotiation.

Common mistakes

Ignoring legitimacy altogether

Negotiators ignore the element of legitimacy at their peril. When negotiators fail to prepare to discuss the rationales of possible agreements, they walk into a negotiation unable to say much more than "Let's agree to this, because it is what I want" (as opposed to explaining why they think what they want to do makes sense or is appropriate). Thus, when the other side resists, the unprepared negotiator can only threaten or pile on concessions to sweeten the deal for the other side. Failing to prepare to discuss objective criteria can be a costly mistake.

Failing to think how your counterpart will explain agreement

Another common oversight is failing to think about how your counterpart will explain the agreement to his or her constituents—be they clients, members of an organization, supervisors, family members, or golf buddies. If you assume that coming up with an acceptable explanation is their problem (as opposed to your responsibility), you risk that they will be unable to do so. Thus they may either not accept an agreement (because it's hard to accept if they can't explain why), or they might accept it but fail to live up to it as they would a deal that they could understand and explain.

Thinking of only one objective rationale

Simply to have thought about an objective rationale for one possible negotiated outcome may not be enough. Just as a little knowledge can be dangerous, preparation that focuses too narrowly, on a single way to justify an agreement, can also be risky. The consequence of this type of preparation mistake is a negotiation that can become positional about the justifications, which is just as problematic as being positional about the solutions. Going into a negotiation convinced that there is only one right answer is a recipe for a tense, adversarial negotiation in which someone wins and someone loses. A well-prepared negotiator has at his or her fingertips a collection of possible principles or criteria that might be used to define a range of reasonable solutions to the issue being negotiated, and several points within that range.

The well-prepared negotiator

Develop a range of fairness

Very few negotiations have only one right answer. The element of legitimacy helps to narrow the range of possibilities to those that treat each side *fairly*. Note that *fairly* does not always mean equally—fair is not always splitting everything down the middle. There are often good reasons why some other arrangement may be appropriate. To be well prepared, you should consider a broad variety of objective criteria that might help you and your counterpart figure out what is appropriate under the circumstances. By looking outside the will of the parties, to external standards or principles, you can avoid getting into a battle over what you will or will not do and discuss what you should do.

Having a variety of standards available to you during the negotiation will help you avoid getting locked into a positional battle over standards. Preparing before the negotiation several possible standards or criteria that might be persuasive to an outsider will also help you become more aware of how your counterpart may be thinking about the situation. And the better you understand where he or she is coming from, the more effective you can be. By being well prepared on a number of different standards, you can also put forward those that are most advantageous to you, yet do so constructively and persuasively.

Consider "fair" processes

It is not always easy to find a principle or a standard that helps you and your counterpart reach agreement. Often, even after using objective criteria to define some outside boundaries to the possible agreement, you are left needing some way to make the final leap from possibilities to a deal. In those situations it pays off to invest time thinking about procedures you might follow that will feel fair.

Think about ways of deciding, as opposed to actual decisions, that have intrinsic appeal to both sides, because they feel reasonable or because they are unlikely to give one side or the other unfair advantage. Sometimes the very things we did as kids to make sure a division was fair have application in our adult lives: "I cut, you choose" or "flipping a coin" have their analogues in business and politics. Agreeing to go to a third party, trusted by both to be impartial, may help parties bridge the final gap between positions backed up by arguments insufficiently persuasive to settle matters. Having thought about how to apply some of these procedures to the case at hand may prove useful if you get stuck.

Prepare to help them explain the result

In your own negotiations, how do you feel about explaining the result by saying "Well, I started by asking for one hundred, but they offered twenty. After much haggling we settled on sixty"? You probably flinch at the thought of the likely response, "Why didn't you start at 150?" or "Why weren't you a bit tougher?" Wouldn't it be much more comfortable to be able to explain the result in terms of industry practices, volume discounts, quality premiums, etc.?

We all have someone to whom we have to explain the result of a negotiation. Sometimes it is our boss or our client, sometimes a spouse, or even our own image in the mirror. We might easily convince ourselves that coming up with explanations for such constituents might be "their problem," not ours, in a negotiation. However, if they do not solve "their problem" well, it does become ours! To whomever it is they respond, if your counterparts cannot give a persuasive explanation for why they accepted the deal they did, it will be difficult, if not impossible, for them to accept it, or once accepted, to comply gracefully and with goodwill. And that is, without a doubt, our problem.

The following three forms can help you get ready to be persuasive.

What specific substantive question has to be answered in this negotiation?

Possible standards (precedents, benchmarks, prior practice, accepted principles, etc.):

Place each standard along a range from least favorable to you to most favorable to you. Below each standard, indicate what that standard would mean in this case.

Least favorable ←———————————————————————————→ **Most favorable**

Standards:

Application
of standard
to this
case:

Other standards that may be relevant or that require research:

Persuasive processes

If you cannot agree on an answer, you might agree on the process to find an agreeable answer. If one of the following looks interesting, how might you apply it to this case?

"I cut, you choose"

Flip a coin

Get an expert opinion

Let an arbitrator decide

The test of reciprocity

In some cases, reciprocity can be very persuasive. Are there some negotiations in which your counterpart is in a position similar to yours?

If so, what standards or arguments does he or she use in the situation?

How could you apply those standards or arguments here?

LEGITIMACY 3: *Offer Them an Attractive Way to Explain Their Decision*

If they had to explain the result of this negotiation to someone important to them, they could convince their constituents with the following few points:

1.

2.

3.

4.

An example

KidWorld Mfg. Co. and the Assembly Workers of America have been negotiating a new three-year contract for weeks. They have successfully resolved a number of issues, reaching tentative agreements on wages, work rules, and performance bonuses. The next issue for discussion, however, promises to be a difficult one.

Health care has become a very sensitive issue around KidWorld. As part of its benefits package for assembly-line workers, KidWorld absorbs approximately 50 percent of workers' health-related costs. This percentage takes into account insurance premiums, co-payments, deductibles, etc. A study done by outside consultants suggested that KidWorld's current health care–related expenses added 12 percent to the cost of every toy sold, a figure approximately four times greater than its overseas competitors. The board is also concerned that health care expenses have increased faster than any cost other than employee wages, which, including performance bonuses, have grown at twice the inflation rate.

The union is also concerned about health care. They have polled their workers and found that the declining purchasing power of their health care dollars ranks second in employee concern preceded only by fears about the security of their pensions. Over the last few years, the company's insurance coverage has failed to keep up with inflation in the health sector, and employee contributions and co-payments have both increased. KidWorld ranks in the top half of employers organized by the Assembly Workers of America in terms of health care benefits but below a significant number of companies similar in size and structure, of its domestic competitors.

The union's negotiation team is preparing to meet with their company counterpart. Traditionally, this issue has been a difficult one to negotiate. The union team has come in asking for the moon (typically full coverage of any and all health-related costs), and the company has come in complaining about how rising health-care costs are making it lose ground to foreign competition. In the last few negotiations, the company has started by seeking to get the union to "give back" some health benefits.

This year, the union has decided to go into the negotiations with something more than bluster and the threat of labor trouble. In addition to thinking hard about possible creative solutions to the problem posed by rising health-care costs, they will also try to bring to the table persuasive standards for dealing with the issue.

What specific substantive question has to be answered in this negotiation?

How much of total cost should company pay?

Possible standards (precedents, benchmarks, prior practice, accepted principles, etc.):

Place each standard along a range from least favorable to you to most favorable to you. Below each standard; indicate what that standard would mean in this case.

	Standards:	Foreign competitors	Peer mfg. co.	KidWorld Current level	U.S. toy cos.	KidHaven Stores	?	
Least favorable ←	Application of standard to this case:	25%	40%	50%	65%	75%	100%	→ Most favorable

Other standards that may be relevant or that require research:

Inflation = 3%/yr   Health care inflation = 12%/yr
Salaried workers at KidWorld = ?
Pension plan matching contribution = 100%
Percentage of total wages employees must devote to health care = ?
Compared to: Salaried workers? Foreign competitors? KidHaven Stores?

LEGITIMACY 2: *Use the Fairness of the Process to Persuade*

Persuasive processes

If you cannot agree on an answer, you might agree on the process to find an agreeable answer. If one of the following looks interesting, how might you apply it to this case?

"I cut, you choose"

Flip a coin

Get an expert opinion

Let an arbitrator decide   Final offer arbitration?   (As in baseball, arbitrator chooses between each side's final offer.)

Most-favored nation   Agree on a number, but if KidWorld gives anyone else a better deal, we get it too.

The test of reciprocity

In some cases, reciprocity can be very persuasive. Are there some negotiations in which your counterpart is in a position similar to yours?

Yes, when negotiating with retailers about co-op advertising.

If so, what standards or arguments does he or she use in the situation?

KidWorld wants a say in how their money is used and an opportunity to get a better deal.

How could you apply those standards or arguments here?

We might say the same things: the union should have a say in how employee contributions are used, and an opportunity to shop around.

LEGITIMACY 3: *Offer Them an Attractive Way to Explain Their Decision*

If they had to explain the result of this negotiation to someone important to them, they could convince their constituents with the following few points:

1. "This is in line with other benefits at KidWorld and with industry practice."

2. "We're holding the line at a level that keeps us competitive."

3. "It's only fair to give employees a chance to participate in deciding how health care dollars are spent for their own benefit. We want the same thing when retailers spend our money on advertising."

4.

As we can see, the Assembly Workers' negotiating team is preparing to meet with their counterparts, the KidWorld Mfg. Co. labor negotiations team. They expect the next round of negotiations to deal with health care benefits, and in particular, to focus on the question of how much of the total cost of health care the company should absorb. Like most issues that can be answered with a number, this is a negotiation that could be very zero-sum and positional. Some standards by which an appropriate answer can be arrived at are likely to be helpful.

Using form **LEGITIMACY 1:** *Use External Standards as a Sword and as a Shield,* the Assembly Workers considered what objective standards could be applied to determine how much of the overall health care cost the company should bear and how much should be left to the workers to deal with. Anchoring one end of the spectrum is probably the benchmark the company is looking to, particularly after the consultant's study that showed how much lower foreign labor costs were. Some of KidWorld's overseas competitors pay as little at 25 percent of the total health care cost of their employees. (Health care is also cheaper in some of these countries, which accounts for the huge difference in the "health care component" of total manufacturing costs.)

At the other end of the spectrum would be 100 percent coverage of all health-related expenses. Unfortunately, the Assembly Workers team could find no objective basis for that position; they will do more research, but as of now, they have no examples of comparable companies in similar industries providing full coverage. Manufacturing companies of about the same size as KidWorld, but not in the toy business, seem to average about 40 percent coverage, whereas other U.S. toy companies average 65 percent. And KidHaven Stores, a highly admired customer, covers 75 percent of its employees' health-related expenses. Still to be researched is the coverage provided by the federal government to its employees. Broadening their search even further, the Assembly Workers' team came up with some additional comparison points, including inflation, health care inflation, and the company's pension plan contribution matching system. Still to be ascertained is the kind of coverage KidWorld provides to its salaried (as opposed to hourly-wage) employees.

Another interesting standard, which will require some additional work to analyze, came from stepping back and thinking about what an outsider would have proposed as a relevant standard. What percentage of their total wages do employees spend for their share of the health-related expenses? This number is in many ways more relevant to the workers, because it tells us how much of their disposable income goes to health care. How does that number compare with the salaried workers at KidWorld? With assembly-line workers at the dreaded foreign competitors? With KidHaven Stores employees?

So far, the preparation has been focused primarily on coming up with objective criteria and quantifiable standards that the KidWorld negotiators might find persuasive as a way to set the percentage of total health-related expenses that the company will pay. These numbers and standards should focus discussion more on the merits and on what the parties should agree to, than on what each is or is not willing to do or to demand from the other. There are also other useful principles that the Assembly Workers' negotiating team could consider applying. We turn to those next on the second form, **LEGITIMACY 2:** *Use the Fairness of the Process to Persuade.*

One avenue for persuasion is to think about the process of deciding. Instead of trying to come up with an answer, we look for agreement on a way of reaching an acceptable answer. As kids we sometimes did this intuitively: "You cut, I choose" was a common way of ensuring the fair distribution of a tasty treat.

When there was no way to split or compromise between two possibilities, flipping a coin sometimes helped leave it to chance as to who would prevail. These and other processes felt fair because they depended on something other than who could bang the table the loudest. They appealed to some fundamental sense of what was fair. What worked then can still work today. Part of good preparation for a difficult negotiation that is likely to get positional around some very concrete issue is to consider what process might seem sufficiently fair to both, that it might serve to overcome an impasse on the substance.

The Assembly Workers found no equivalent to "I cut, you choose" or flipping a coin, but they did think that "final offer arbitration" might be appealing as a last resort. Final offer arbitration is a process by which each side submits to a neutral arbitrator (someone both sides can accept) its final, binding offer to resolve a negotiation issue along with an explanation of why that offer is appropriate. The arbitrator then is required to choose one of the two, rather than split the difference. This process is designed to encourage the parties to submit reasonable final offers, or else run the risk that one side's offer will seem more "reasonable" than a more extreme offer.

The Assembly Workers also found another potential persuasive process for agreement: the parties might agree to a particular health care cost contribution but also agree that the Assembly Workers will be entitled to "most favored nation" status—that is, if KidWorld, in negotiations with other unions (transport, office workers, maintenance workers, etc.), gives anyone else a better health care package, the Assembly Workers' package will be adjusted.

As you prepare to negotiate with someone, it is useful to think about possible situations in which your counterpart's shoe is on the other foot. With whom do they negotiate, and about what, when they are in a position similar to the one you are in with respect to them? For example, every company that sells also buys. Most managers have someone they have to account to for their performance. If you can figure out what that "other foot" is for your counterpart, and think about what principles they like to see applied in those negotiations, you may find a very persuasive standard to apply in yours (this is generally called the "standard of reciprocity").

The Assembly Workers had some trouble with this part of their preparation. It is not easy to imagine KidWorld seeking to have someone pay for part of a benefit they need. The closest example they could come up with was cooperative advertising: large retailers, like KidHaven Stores, expect manufacturers to pay for some of the advertising of their products by the retailer. In the very competitive business KidWorld finds itself in, the largest of retailers have tremendous bargaining power, and they tend to tell manufacturers what their share of the advertising costs will be, yet give the manufacturers very little say in how that money is spent. Many a time the Assembly Worker negotiators have heard KidWorld executives complain about how little influence they have in the use of their money. The executives think that if they had more of a role, they might be able to get better value for their expenditure. Although the situation is at best a distant analogy, it does suggest a principle that could be applied to health care negotiations, with which the KidWorld team may be able to sympathize: currently Assembly Workers' representatives have no say in how health care dollars are spent. The company chooses the coverage, negotiates the rates, and informs the workers that it is covering 50 percent of that cost. It may be that if the Assembly Workers negotiated rates with several insurance companies and health care providers, they might be able to use the clout that comes from being 250,000 members strong to negotiate a better rate than KidWorld can get for its 10,000 employees.

The final part of preparing to persuade requires thinking about how the other side might be able to explain the outcome. In particular, it is useful to think about how the other side will be able to describe the agreement to its constituents, superiors, or peers. Using **LEGITIMACY 3: *Offer Them an Attractive Way to Explain Their Decision,*** the Assembly Workers found it easy to come up with an explanation to relatively impartial observers; it took more effort to come up with a possible explanation to satisfy the current CEO and board of directors because it required some reference to the company's competitiveness. Working to come up with these explanations suggested to the Assembly Workers that the deal itself will have to include some element of productivity gain or some other tie-in to the competitiveness of the company. Without this, the KidWorld negotiators are unlikely to be able to sell it to their constituents.

CHAPTER 7

Communication

Am I Ready to Listen and Talk Effectively?

Process is important. It can change outright antagonism between two nego-tiatiors into a win/win feeling and vice versa. It can transform what seemed like a simple decision into a bureaucratic nightmare, or shape a messy situation with lots of different parties into something manageable where progress is possible.

While process may be too broad a term to think about as you prepare to negotiate, you can focus on two important aspects of process, which are them-selves closely related: (1) How do we communicate with the other side? and (2) How do we manage our working relationship? In this chapter, we'll take up the first challenge: good communication. We'll address how to prepare to build a good working relationship in **Chapter 8.**

As we negotiate, we should strive for good communication. Good commu-nication tends to eliminate misunderstandings and to make our negotiations proceed more efficiently. With good communication, negotiations become a process that makes it easier, rather than harder, to deal with each other in the future. Preparation can help us accomplish these goals. Because a well-prepared negotiator thinks carefully about how the other side might see the sit-uation and about what concerns they might have about our intentions, he or she is ready to deal with potential differences, and to do so in a way that brings the parties closer together rather than pushing them further apart.

Common mistakes

Focusing on rehearsing lines

When negotiators spend most of their energy thinking about what they are going to say to the other side, they are most likely to say the wrong thing. One of
the most common preparation mistakes is to focus on rehearsing lines. Comforting as it may be, such rehearsal tends to limit our ability to do something
much more important: to listen and to understand. The problem is not so much
one of rigidity—sticking to the prepared text even after it is discovered to be irrelevant or obsolete—but one of perspective and attention. If you get ready by
thinking about what you will say, you will tend to be unprepared for what they
have to say or for how they might interpret what you do say.

Ignoring blind spots

At any given time, a negotiator can perceive only a part of the whole puzzle of
interactions, perceptions, and intentions. As we act, we tend to be aware of our
own intentions and our own perceptions. But we simply cannot know how our
our words or actions will be perceived by them or what impact they will have.
Similarly, when we listen and observe, we can try to be aware of what they say
and do, how we perceive that, and what impact it has on us. But try as we
might, we cannot know their intentions or their perceptions.

These limitations do not themselves keep us from being effective negotiators. But ignoring them and acting as if we could be certain about their intentions, or certain how our actions have an impact on them, will interfere with
our ability to work effectively together.

The well-prepared negotiator

Prepare for two-way communication

The traditional advice to negotiators is to listen carefully. Regardless of intentions or favored tactics, listening to the other side, so that you can then make
good choices about what to do and how to do it, is universally important. What
negotiators often neglect, however, is preparing to listen. Extensive research
into how people communicate demonstrates that the ability to listen can be im-

paired by anything from the assumptions brought to the discussion to distractions that occur during it. If we fail to invest some effort in the listening process, both before and during, we tend to hear what we want to hear, rather than what our counterpart is intending to communicate.

As you prepare to negotiate, it is important to think about what you expect them to say—and how you would recognize a different message. Otherwise, your assumptions are likely to make it difficult, if not impossible, to hear anything else. If you find yourself thinking something like "There is just nothing he can say that I'd be willing to believe," then it is time to reconsider your upcoming meeting and find another way to communicate—perhaps through actions instead of words or with the help of an intermediary.

Similarly, to be effective during a negotiation you should prepare to deliver messages so they can hear them. This requires some thinking about how they might interpret your statements through the filters of their own assumptions and biases. It may require reframing statements so that you actually communicate what you intend. This calls for a greater effort, but what is the alternative? If you state things in a way that is likely to be misheard, your communication will not serve its intended purpose.

The following two forms are designed to help you prepare for effective communication.

The first step in dealing with your blind spots is to become aware of them. In the left-hand column, list your assumptions about their intentions and perceptions. In the right-hand column, write down key phrases your counterpart might say that should lead you to question your assumptions.

My assumptions (I assume that . . .)	Things to listen for

Your perspective	How might they hear it?	Reframing
(List 3–5 statements you might make to clearly put forth your interests.)	(For each statement, list your counterpart's possible response, e.g., "Yes, but . . .")	(Restate your interests so that they will hear them better.)

An example

Because both communication and relationship are elements that focus on the process of the interaction between negotiators, we will use the same example in the **Communication** and **Relationship** chapters.

Doris has had a running argument with her landlord, Pedro, for the last few months. She wants him to paint her apartment and make some minor cosmetic repairs, and he refuses. Doris is quite unhappy about the situation—enough so to consider moving out. That would be a tremendous hassle right now, given everything else that is going on at work and with her family.

Doris has been living in this apartment for about two years. The apartment is great in almost every respect—good neighborhood, conveniently located, spacious. She was quite pleased with herself when she found it, and she accepted what was for her a relatively high rent, deciding it was worth it to have a home she really liked. Because Pedro had painted the apartment the year before, Doris did not insist on the usual between-tenants paint job; it was also more convenient to take the apartment as soon as it became available. But it is now two years later, and a couple of rooms are really showing wear. In fact, Doris has had to rearrange some bookshelves and move some framed prints around to try to hide peeling paint in places where apparently moisture and temperature changes (the building seems not to be very well insulated, and the windows are old and a bit drafty) have done the worst damage.

The first time she asked Pedro if he would have the apartment painted, Pedro gave her the brush-off. When she insisted a few weeks later, he became quite agitated, complaining that he wasn't made of money and telling Doris not to be so fussy. Surprised by the reaction from her normally pleasant and polite landlord, Doris backed off. In fact, whenever she had previously asked Pedro to fix little things (bad light switch, stopped-up sink) he had done so without argument. But she continued to be unhappy by the look of her apartment, and after one of her friends commented on the peeling, Doris went back to Pedro. This time he was even more emotional and became verbally abusive, suggesting that if there was anything wrong, it was probably her own fault and that she should not expect him to fix what she had damaged.

Doris has decided that she does not just want to leave things as they are. She wants her apartment painted, and she wants to be able to get along well with her landlord for the future. She has decided that before approaching Pedro again, however, she wants to prepare more carefully to deal with the surprisingly emotional reaction she has gotten so far and to improve their communication.

COMMUNICATION 1: *Question My Assumptions and Identify Things to Listen For*

NEGOTIATOR: Doris
COUNTERPART: Pedro
SUBJECT: Painting/repairs

The first step in dealing with your blind spots is to become aware of them. In the left-hand column, list your assumptions about their intentions and perceptions. In the right-hand column, write down key phrases your counterpart might say that should lead you to question your assumptions.

My assumptions (I assume that . . .)	Things to listen for
Pedro's intentions 　-hostile 　-unwilling to spend money	Questions about extent/location of damage Questions about what it might cost Asking to see the damage
Pedro's perceptions of me 　-Thinks I'm a pain and that I'm trying to take advantage of him	I don't know
Pedro wants me to move out?	Asking about my willingness to sign a longer lease Questions about my future plans Statement that he can't be painting the apartment every other year
Pedro thinks he can push me around?	Asking whether the apartment is OK in other ways Willingness to explore options

COMMUNICATION 2: *Reframe to Help Them Understand*

Your perspective (List 3–5 statements you might make to clearly put forth your interests.)	**How might they hear it?** (For each statement, list your counterpart's possible response, e.g., "Yes, but . . .")	**Reframing** (Restate your interests so that they will hear them better.)
1. I am embarrassed by peeling paint.	a. It's not so bad. b. Doris is probably responsible for the damage.	1. Apt. in general is great; but condition of a few rooms is quite bad, possibly because of moisture.
2. I pay a lot of rent.	a. Market rate b. I'm not getting rich from this!	2. Apt. is in moderate to high end of market; shouldn't that mean mod. to high end of maintenance?
3. I've lived here 2 years and I haven't asked for much.	a. Standard is 5 years between paint jobs. b. I'm a good landlord—I've always fixed anything she asked for.	3. Normal practice is 5 years or change of tenants. In this case it has been 3 years and change of tenant, and an unusual winter moisture problem that has damaged some rooms more than normal wear and tear. How should we deal with that?
4. I gave you a break when I moved in without insisting you repaint.	a. It didn't need it!	4. I've never been one to insist on technicalities; when a paint job wasn't necessary, I agreed to do without. But now I think the apartment needs some work.

In this case, what looks like a relatively simple negotiation over painting an apartment has become complicated by communication difficulties. Rather than blaming the communication problem on Pedro, Doris begins by focusing on what she can do to improve things. In the left-hand column of the form **COMMUNICATION 2: *Reframe to Help Them Understand*** Doris has outlined the key things she would say to Pedro about why he should fix and paint her apartment. In the middle column, she has done something we sometimes find it difficult to do: she has tried to put herself in Pedro's shoes and imagine what he might think or say—not about the whole issue—but about each of Doris's points. These are only Doris's guesses about what Pedro might think; but those guesses allow her to make the best use of the information she has and to understand a little better what Pedro may be thinking.

The right-hand column is where Doris develops her new communication strategy. Having some sense of how Pedro might react to the statements she was planning, Doris can now reframe or restate her points, so that it is easier for Pedro to hear them without reacting emotionally. By making her statements in terms of the issues Pedro considers relevant, Doris ensures that her arguments are harder to dismiss. For example, instead of complaining about being embarrassed—suggesting Pedro's property is substandard or an eyesore—she acknowledges that the apartment is generally fine, but that something outside her control (moisture) has caused some problems. Similarly, instead of complaining that the rent is high—to which Pedro's responses are fairly predictable—Doris asks a question about what's reasonable in the "moderate to high end" of the market.

This type of framing is likely to force Pedro to think, instead of react. Statements or questions that begin with, or refer to, issues people care about are more likely to be listened to, instead of being dismissed as irrelevant noise. Statements or questions that can't be answered with automatic reactions improve the quality of communication and decision making.

In order to be able to hear well what the other side is saying, we need to think about what we expect to hear, and about what else we might try to listen for. In order to manage our blind spots, we need to be aware of our assumptions. Here, using the form **COMMUNICATION 1: *Question My Assumptions and Identify Things to Listen For,*** Doris has realized that she expects Pedro to be hostile to her request and unwilling to spend money on her apartment. That, after all, is how he reacted on previous occasions. She assumes he perceives her as difficult and trying to take advantage of him.

It is difficult for Doris to imagine what other reaction Pedro will have. But as she thinks about it, it occurs to her that perhaps he has signaled other intentions by asking about the nature of the damage. He might do that by asking to see it or offer some guess as to the cost of repairing it. As to Pedro's perceptions, she really draws a blank—how might Pedro act if he doesn't think she's trying to take advantage of him?

CHAPTER 8

Relationship

Am I Ready to Deal with the Relationship?

A critical element in any negotiation—and one that frequently causes the most anxiety—is the quality of the working relationship we have with the other side. A good working relationship enables us to handle our differences efficiently. A bad working relationship can scuttle a deal even when, at least on paper, both parties could have been better off had they agreed. We need not like each other or even share values or interests. But so long as we find ourselves negotiating, we would like to use a process that enables us to handle our differences well *this* time and makes it easier to negotiate the next time.

The quality of a relationship is not just something that happens. It is the product of how we deal with each other. The well-prepared negotiator thinks about how we *ought* to deal with each other and then plans steps to carry us in that direction. To build an effective working relationship, such steps should increase mutual understanding, build trust and respect, encourage mutual persuasion (rather than coercion), enable us to keep reason and emotion in balance, and, of course, enhance communication.

Common mistakes

Confusing relationship and substance

Among the most common—and most human—errors negotiators tend to make is to lump together the people and the problem. That is, we tend to confuse matters of relationship—how we deal with disagreement, hurt feelings, etc.—

with those of substance—numbers, dates, terms, and conditions. Failing to distinguish between the two as we get ready to negotiate is likely to leave us trying to fix a relationship by making substantive concessions, and *vice versa*. Neither will work. If we have a relationship problem—for example, lack of trust or respect—trying to deal with it by dropping our price or agreeing to accept their conditions on some substantive term will not remedy that problem. On the contrary, it may well teach them that to get concessions from us, all they need to do is act hurt or distrustful.

Assuming that the relationship is a "given" and that "It's their fault!"

Perhaps because we spend the first years of our lives in relationships over which we have little control, many negotiators tend to treat their relationship with the other negotiator as something that "just occurs," a product of the situation. If the relationship sours, our usual response may be to blame the other side. In either case, we may assume that there is little we can do to improve the situation. If there is little we can do anyway, then why prepare? That line of thinking creates a self-fulfilling prophecy and we do, indeed, exercise little control over the quality of our relationships.

The well-prepared negotiator

Prepare to address relationship and substance independently

You cannot cure hurt feelings with substantive concessions, any more than you can make up for a significant loss of money with an apology. Nor should you attempt to do so. If you allow substantive and relationship problems to become mixed up, you confuse matters and undermine both your relationship—treating it as if it were for sale, or allowing it to be held hostage to some substantive term—*and* your ability to negotiate a deal on the merits.

In order to keep relationship and substantive issues separate during a negotiation and to deal with each of them well, you'll need to identify which are "substantive" issues or problems and which are "relationship" or "people" problems. Substantive problems pertain to the content of the negotiation—price, terms, conditions, dates, and so forth. Substantive issues tend to be those that we think should "be resolved" by the end of the negotiation. On the other hand, relationship issues tend to affect *the negotiation itself;* we may feel we need to deal with them in order to reach agreement on the substantive issues. Whether management will cover all the employees' health insurance costs is a substantive issue. The insults that labor and management may be trading in the newspaper involve relationship. Keeping these two lists separate will help you make sure that you address both types of concerns, without trading off one against the other in ways that will be troublesome in the long term.

Prepare to take unconditionally constructive steps to improve the relationship

Once you have identified the substantive and relationship issues, you'll need to think about how to deal with them. For the substantive problems, you'll need to be well prepared on interests, options, legitimacy, alternatives, and commitments. For the relationship issues, you'll need to think about steps that you can take that will help improve the relationship, whether or not the other side reciprocates. Any steps you take should be "unconditionally constructive"—that is, you should do those things that are good for you *and* help improve the relationship, whether or not the other side reciprocates.

By deciding to be "unconditional" we take responsibility and, to some extent, control over the quality of our working relationship. We focus on what *we* can do to improve the relationship, instead of feeling powerless because *they* are being negative. By making sure we are "constructive," we look to build the relationship on a solid foundation. That foundation should take into account our interests and should help aim the relationship in a direction in which we would like it to continue. So we do not simply "give in" for the sake of the relationship. We take action to get on the right footing.[*]

The following two forms will help you prepare to deal with the relationship.

---

[*]For more information on the "unconditionally constructive" strategy to building working relationships, see Roger Fisher and Scott Brown, *Getting Together: Building Relationships as We Negotiate* (New York: Penguin, 1989).

RELATIONSHIP 1: *Separate People Issues from Substantive Issues*

NEGOTIATOR: _____

COUNTERPART: _____

SUBJECT: _____

Describe your relationship. (Use adjectives.)

Separate the relationship from the substance

Substantive issues and problems	**Relationship issues and problems**
(money, terms, dates, and conditions)	(reliability, mutual acceptance, emotions, etc.)

Substantive options and remedies	**Ways to improve the relationship**
(Consider referring to the chapters on **Interests** and **Options.**)	(Make sure these are not substantive concessions.)

RELATIONSHIP 2: *Prepare to Build a Good Working Relationship*

NEGOTIATOR: _____

COUNTERPART: _____

SUBJECT: _____

What might be wrong now?	What can *I* do . . .
What might be causing any present mis-understanding?	. . . to try to understand them better?
What might be causing a lack of trust?	. . . to demonstrate my reliability?
What might be causing one or both of us to feel coerced?	. . . to put the focus on persuasion instead of coercion?
What might be causing one or both of us to feel disrespected?	. . . to show acceptance and respect?
What might be causing one or both of us to get upset?	. . . to balance emotion and reason?

An example

Because both communication and relationship are elements that focus on the process of the interaction between negotiators, we will use the same example in the **Communication** and **Relationship** chapters.

Doris has had a running argument with her landlord, Pedro, for the last few months. She wants him to paint her apartment and make some minor cosmetic repairs, and he refuses. Doris is quite unhappy about the situation—enough so to consider moving out. That would be a tremendous hassle right now, given everything else that is going on at work and with her family.

Doris has been living in this apartment for about two years. The apartment is great in almost every respect—good neighborhood, conveniently located, spacious. She was quite pleased with herself when she found it, and she accepted what was for her a relatively high rent, deciding it was worth it to have a home she really liked. Because Pedro had painted the apartment the year before, Doris did not insist on the usual between-tenants paint job; it was also more convenient to take the apartment as soon as it became available. But it is now two years later, and a couple of rooms are really showing wear. In fact, Doris has had to rearrange some bookshelves and move some framed prints around to try to hide peeling paint in places where apparently moisture and temperature changes (the building seems not to be very well insulated, and the windows are old and a bit drafty) have done the worst damage.

The first time she asked Pedro if he would have the apartment painted, Pedro gave her the brush-off. When she insisted a few weeks later, he became quite agitated, complaining that he wasn't made of money and telling Doris not to be so fussy. Surprised by the reaction from her normally pleasant and polite landlord, Doris backed off. In fact, whenever she had previously asked Pedro to fix little things (bad light switch, stopped-up sink) he had done so without argument. But she continued to be unhappy by the look of her apartment, and after one of her friends commented on the peeling, Doris went back to Pedro. This time he was even more emotional and became verbally abusive, suggesting that if there was anything wrong, it was probably her own fault and that she should not expect him to fix what she had damaged.

Doris has decided that she does not just want to leave things as they are. She wants her apartment painted, and she wants to be able to get along well with her landlord for the future. She has decided that before approaching Pedro again, however, she wants to prepare more carefully to deal with the surprisingly emotional reaction she has gotten so far and to improve their communication.

RELATIONSHIP 1: *Separate People Issues from Substantive Issues*

NEGOTIATOR: <u>Doris</u>

COUNTERPART: <u>Pedro</u>

SUBJECT: <u>Painting/repairs</u>

Describe your relationship. (Use adjectives.)

Difficult, emotional about this issue.

Separate the relationship from the substance

Substantive issues and problems (money, terms, dates, and conditions)	**Relationship issues and problems** (reliability, mutual acceptance, emotions, etc.)
Cost of paint	Poor communication
Labor	Personal attack
Number of years between paint jobs	Blaming
Amount of rent	

Substantive options and remedies (Consider referring to the chapters on **Interests** and **Options**.)	**Ways to improve the relationship** (Make sure these are not substantive concessions.)
Paint only problem areas	Meet to talk about other things
Paint now, and sign a longer lease (2–3 years?)	Focus on future instead of past
Fix windows, etc., that caused damage	Ask questions
Share cost	Listen and paraphrase back
Do the work together over a weekend	Invite Pedro to look and ask for help figuring out the cause of the problem

RELATIONSHIP 2: *Prepare to Build a Good Working Relationship*

NEGOTIATOR: Doris

COUNTERPART: Pedro

SUBJECT: Painting/repairs

What might be wrong now?	What can *I* do . . .
What might be causing any present misunderstanding?	**. . . to try to understand them better?**
Disagreement about causes of the problem Never been in each other's shoes	Ask more questions Talk to other landlords about typical concerns
What might be causing a lack of trust?	**. . . to demonstrate my reliability?**
	Invite him to look over apartment to show everything else is OK
What might be causing one or both of us to feel coerced?	**. . . to put the focus on persuasion instead of coercion?**
Talk about moving out	Ask for advice about what to do with peeling paint until Pedro paints
What might be causing one or both of us to feel disrespected?	**. . . to show acceptance and respect?**
What might be causing one or both of us to get upset?	**. . . to balance emotion and reason?**
Defensive reaction	Keep my cool Reframe issues

DATE PREPARED: _____

In this case, Doris is negotiating directly with Pedro, her landlord. In thinking about her working relationship with Pedro, she has noted that the difficulties center mostly on the paint issue. She is worried about the way in which this discussion might affect an otherwise cordial relationship and, therefore, make it difficult for her to stay in the apartment.

This situation, like so many others, has elements of substance (money, numbers, dates, legal or other norms, etc.) and relationship (respect, trust, communication, etc.). Separating them as called for by the form **RELATIONSHIP 1:** *Separate People Issues from Substantive Issues* allows Doris to think of substantive solutions to substantive problems (for example, painting the problem areas or fixing the drafty windows) and relationship solutions to relationship problems (for example, meeting to talk about ways to improve communication or asking Pedro to help figure out what is causing the problem instead of blaming).

Once Doris has sorted out the problems in this way, she can see the situation more clearly and avoid confusing how she and Pedro deal with each other and their differences with what they might do about them.

In working through **RELATIONSHIP 2:** *Prepare to Build a Good Working Relationship,* Doris notices some ways in which she may be contributing to the difficult interaction, by her own lack of understanding of what it is like to be a landlord, by resorting to a threat of moving out or by getting defensive when Pedro gets angry. Although she has no intention of simply "giving in" on the issue, she finds she can be more effective if she works somewhat at dealing with Pedro better **as a person.**

CHAPTER 9

Commitment

What Commitments Should I Seek or Make?

Often we prepare for a negotiation by thinking about where to begin. Good negotiators begin by thinking about where they would like to end up. This understanding enables them to chart out a path for getting there.

At the conclusion of a negotiation, unless they decide to walk away, the parties make *commitments*. These are agreements about what each party will actually do. For a negotiation to be considered successful, those commitments should be clear, well planned, and durable.

Only by having a clear notion of what kinds of commitments would be desirable as the end product of each meeting and of the negotiation as a whole can negotiators be fully proactive and purposive. Knowing where you would like to end up is not the same as having a negotiation position fixed in your mind; nor should it mean having an inflexible bottom line. But understanding whether the purpose of the next meeting is to reach a final agreement or simply to explore some possible options will make a big difference in what you discuss and how you discuss it. Similarly, knowing that a workable deal must address not only price, but also delivery and pay-ment terms, and that it must set out a process for controlling quality and managing the inevitable disagreements that will arise, will make it more likely that when you are ready to reach a final agreement you will have adequately discussed all the terms that will determine whether or not your negotiation really is a success.

Common mistakes

Not knowing what "done" looks like

Many negotiations begin by having the parties name an issue or two they need to resolve—price and delivery date, for example. Over the course of the nego-tiation, they discover (if they are lucky) a number of other issues that, if ig-nored, could undermine their agreement—such as form of shipment, insurance, quality assurance, payment terms, etc. If they fail to discuss how they will ad-dress some of these issues and, perhaps, some contingencies like unavoidable delays or even the need to cancel the order, each side will simply do as they see fit. The consequences may be a damaged relationship and a deal that is not very durable.

Assuming everyone knows what the meeting is about

Another common mistake in preparation is to assume that "everyone knows" what the meeting is about and that, therefore, they are in agreement about what should be accomplished. A common assumption that a negotiation is to be about "how to deal with this problem" may not mean that everyone agrees that the product of the meeting should be an action plan. For some, a good re-sult of the negotiation may simply be that information is shared and that a date and time are set for a future meeting. Although there is no "right answer" about what the product of each meeting should be, plunging ahead with untested as-sumptions can leave everyone frustrated.

Failing to determine actions needed to reach agreement

Negotiators sometimes fail to think carefully through the sequence of events that will be required to reach an agreement that is ready for implementation. Just because you have authority to commit your side, and you are meeting with someone who also seems to have that capacity, does not mean either that the meeting *should* result in a final accord or that if you do reach one, it can be smoothly (if at all) put into action. We often fail to remember that a "decision" does not always translate into action—if the necessary steps have not been thought through and if those whose collaboration is required have not been considered or consulted.

The well-prepared negotiator

Plan ahead for operational commitments

Without knowing precisely what you and your counterpart will agree to, you should be able to come up with a relatively complete list of issues you expect will need to be addressed in the negotiation. If you were to think of the complete agreement as a book, these would be the chapter titles. What are the questions for which you will need to come up with some answer for the deal to work? If you can prepare such a list in advance of the negotiation—remaining open, of course, to modifying it during the negotiation—you will have a checklist of issues to discuss and a way to ensure that loose ends eventually get dealt with and tied down.

The more complex the negotiation, the less you want to leave the details to chance. Thus, for complicated business negotiations, you should take your list of issues and consider what it will actually take to implement whatever your agreement turns out to be. In particular, you should think, issue by issue, about who will have to give approval not just formally, but practically, for something to get done; when you expect to see signs that the agreement is being implemented; and how you will measure or recognize successful implementation. This kind of advance preparation will make your negotiation process more effective and the implementation of any commitments go more smoothly.

Clarify the purpose, product, and process of your meetings

If you have ever sat in a meeting and felt you were wasting time, it is almost certainly because its participants were not well prepared. They may have each brought with them lots of information, skills, and interest in helping. But if no one devoted some advance thought to the purpose of the meeting, and no one made any effort to make sure that all its attendees understood that purpose, chances are the meeting was doomed from the start.

As you get ready to negotiate, spend some time up front clarifying the purpose of the meeting—Why are you getting together? How will you know whether the meeting was successful? One way to make your purpose clearer and more tangible is to specify what product you hope to have in hand by the end of the meeting. Is it a document? A decision to take action? A set of questions to think about? Once you know why you are meeting and what you hope to accomplish, you can more effectively plan the process for your meeting—an agenda, some ground rules, even a sense of the kind of space or equipment you might need.

Plan the process for getting to a commitment

Some negotiations start and end in one meeting, and the negotiators themselves can and do make all the relevant decisions and commitments. Others, particularly in the worlds of business and public policy, are much more complex. Reaching a good outcome requires not only a series of meetings at which the issues can be discussed but also a number of activities before and after each meeting, to ensure that the necessary information is collected, the right people are consulted, and potential pitfalls are explored. Managing that sequence of interactions, some on our side, some on theirs, requires the kind of coordination and communication that can be achieved only with good advance preparation.

As you get ready for a negotiation or for subsequent meetings in an extended negotiation, it is often useful to prepare a one-sided draft of a possible final agreement. This may not be complete. It may not be a proposal that you will make to the other side. It will, however, stimulate clear thinking about the kind of commitments you might like and can realistically expect. Also, take some time to think not only about *what* will have to be included in your deal for the commitment to be durable and operational, but *how* you will be able to put together that commitment. What steps will be required? Who will have to agree in order to move from one stage of the process to the next? Who will make the final decision? What kind of information, tools, people, or resources will be necessary to accomplish the various tasks—including communicating effectively with the other side and with interested bystanders, brainstorming possible creative solutions, researching objective standards to help us resolve difficult issues, and exploring our walk-away alternative. It is often useful to attempt to draw a diagram of the various activities or events that will be required for the negotiation to be successful, and attempt to list what may be required for each activity. If you can put all this on a realistic timeline, you are more likely to be able to tackle the complexity of the negotiation head-on and manage the process constructively.

Use the forms that follow to help plan your commitments.

COMMITMENT 1: *Identify the Issues to Be Included in the Agreement*

NEGOTIATOR: _____

COUNTERPART: _____

SUBJECT: _____

Overall purpose of negotiation

Expected product of negotiation

(Draft a table of contents for a final agreement that would be operational and durable.)

Specific purpose of next meeting

Tangible product of next meeting

(If you could imagine the piece of paper you would produce during *this* meeting, what would it contain?)

___ A list of options for further consideration?

___ An action plan for further work necessary before an agreement would be possible?

___ A joint recommendation to your respective organizations?

___ An agreement in principle?

___ A signed contract?

___ Commitments toward the next steps?

___ Other _____

COMMITMENT 2: *Plan the Steps to Agreement*

NEGOTIATOR: _____

COUNTERPART: _____

SUBJECT: _____

Decision makers: names of those who will "sign" the agreement

Implementation: information that the agreement should include about what happens next

Implementors who should perhaps be consulted before agreement is final:

Possible obstacles to implementation:

Ways to deal with obstacles:

Steps necessary to get to a binding agreement

Target date

1. Tentative agreement on issues to be included: _____

2. Clarification of interests on each issue: _____

3. Discussion of options for handling each issue: _____

4. My draft of a framework agreement: _____

5. Joint working draft of possible agreement: _____

6. Final text ready for signature: _____

An example

Mark has been leading the TrueLab negotiating team in their discussions with Advantage Software over a possible joint venture to combine TrueLab's expertise in designing and manufacturing laboratory diagnostic equipment with Advantage's artificial intelligence software. Their technical teams believe that such a combination could create an exciting new expert system to automate much of the routine work conducted by medical laboratories. Discussions have gone on for the better part of six months, and Mark is under pressure from top management to bring them to fruition soon, before the potential market lead that the joint venture would have over competitors evaporates.

Mark also thinks that it is about time to cut through the final issues and reach closure. He is hoping that the day and half of meetings he has scheduled at Advantage's offices in San Jose will prove sufficient. He would like to return to TrueLab headquarters in Boston with a done deal—or at least with something that is definite and clear enough that it can be turned over to the lawyers to write up without giving them much room to renegotiate the deal and gum up the works.

After months of discussions, with input from technical and finance staff, the negotiating teams have worked out a nicely balanced package of initial contributions from each side to the joint venture (patents, staff, market knowledge and presence, cash, etc.). Mark and his counterpart at Advantage both seem to feel this package meets each side's interests in having its contributions fairly recognized and in sharing equally in the venture. They have also arrived at a basic understanding of the market in which the venture would operate and, with the help of outside consultants, developed some idea of its size and potential. The basic governance structure of the joint venture is set, but its management team remains to be identified. Also on Mark's list as "open" issues are: (1) how to avoid having all the venture's business come at the expense of TruéLab's existing offerings; (2) how to deal with the significant differences in culture between the two companies; and (3) what to name the new venture.

Before returning his CEO's call asking whether he thought they might wrap things up this week, Mark spent a few minutes planning for this next (and, he hopes, final) round of negotiations.

Overall purpose of negotiation

Establish joint venture with Advantage Software

Expected product of negotiation

(Draft a table of contents for a final agreement that would be operational and durable.)

1. Name of joint venture

2. Joint venture purpose, business definition, and limits

3. Contributions of each partner

4. Joint venture structure
   a) equity shares
   b) board of directors
   c) management process

5. Action plan for integration
   a) timetable
   b) staff
   c) location
   d) budgeting
   e) relationship building among new team members

Specific purpose of next meeting

Wrap up open issues and reach agreement

Tangible product of next meeting

(If you could imagine the piece of paper you would produce during *this* meeting, what would it contain?)

____ A list of options for further consideration?

____ An action plan for further work necessary before an agreement would be possible?

____ A joint recommendation to your respective organizations?

____ An agreement in principle?

____ A signed contract?

____ Commitments toward the next steps?

✓ Other ___a term sheet_____

COMMITMENT 2: *Plan the Steps to Agreement*

NEGOTIATOR: Mark
COUNTERPART: Advantage team
SUBJECT: Joint venture

Decision makers: names of those who will "sign" the agreement

CEO of each company

Implementation: information that the agreement should include about what happens next

Implementors who should perhaps be consulted before agreement is final:

Engineering, Marketing, Research, Customer

Possible obstacles to implementation:

Customer resistance?
FDA regulations?

Ways to deal with obstacles:

?

Steps necessary to get to a binding agreement	Target date
1. Tentative agreement on issues to be included:	Mostly Done
2. Clarification of interests on each issue:	Partially Done
3. Discussion of options for handling each issue:	Partially Done
4. My draft of a framework agreement:	?
5. Joint working draft of possible agreement:	?
6. Final text ready for signature:	?

Mark's purposes seem pretty clear: he was asked to lead this negotiating team to explore a possible joint venture that TrueLab's strategic planning department had identified as important to the company's future, and that the two CEOs had agreed made sense to pursue. Although he would not want to do a bad deal, he is out to see whether a good one is feasible.

For this next meeting, Mark has a very specific purpose in mind: finish the business side of the negotiations and turn things over to the Legal Department. As he thought about how that purpose translated into a tangible product, it seemed to him that what he wanted was what is known as a "term sheet"— a substantive outline of all the business and technical terms agreed to in the deal, which just needs to be put into binding contractual language without further ado.

His thinking of what the outline should cover is shown in the center section of **COMMITMENT 1:** *Identify the Issues to Be Included in the Agreement.* These items are basically what he and the Advantage negotiators have been discussing over the last few meetings. Mark is fairly comfortable with the way most of these have been resolved, and there are only a few open questions in his mind.

The final part of careful planning for this meeting is to think about whether a deal that covered all the items in his table of contents would be operational— in other words, easy to implement, with responsibilities clearly assigned, time frames defined, and visible milestones of progress staked out—as well as durable, capable of withstanding differences in assumptions and unforeseen events. For this, he turned to **COMMITMENT 2:** *Plan the Steps to an Agreement.*

As Mark thought through some of these questions, a few things occurred to him. First of all, at TrueLab, the final decision on this deal would be made by his CEO, and he assumed the same would be true at Advantage. Therefore, a signed term sheet may not be possible: at best, he may be able to bring back something that the two negotiation teams have agreed to and will recommend to their respective CEOs. Second, considering how important the cooperation of other departments might be, he should probably spend some time meeting with them before he flies out to San Jose. Third, he noticed with some trepidation that neither he nor his counterpart had spent any time discussing how to deal with potential barriers like customer resistance or regulatory delays that may affect how quickly they can come to market. Although these are issues that the joint venture's management could eventually grapple with on their own, the failure to have discussed them up front could lead to a messy round of blaming later; some prior discussion might help the partners figure out whether there is something they can do to minimize the potential problems up front (if not, the venture might be doomed to failure from the start!).

Reflecting on these questions, Mark realized he had a lot to do before he could promise his CEO that he could wrap up the deal next week. He began by calling his counterpart at Advantage, to review some of his thinking on issues that still needed attention and to discuss a timetable for getting them resolved.

Moving from Preparation to Negotiation

CHAPTER 10

Getting Ready to Agree

Chapter by chapter, we have made some suggestions about why certain preparation steps would be useful to you and how you might use the information you gather in the forms to negotiate more effectively. Yet we imagine there may remain some doubts about how to go forward and what to do next.

One useful place to start would be to review your copy of *Getting to Yes*. The advice contained within that book should help you picture more vividly what you might say or do in your negotiations. This workbook is intended to help you *get ready* to follow the advice in *Getting to Yes*.

As you try to assemble the results of your preparation and gather your thoughts about where and how to begin, we recommend that you approach the first part of the negotiation as if it were just another kind of preparation. Instead of *preparing to negotiate* by yourself, you should think of your next step as *preparing to agree* jointly with your counterpart.

What does this mean precisely? How does one prepare jointly with the other side? And what about confidential information? There is no magic formula guaranteeing you that your negotiation will get off on the right foot and that you will say "the right thing" every time. Yet, we think that the frame of mind you bring to the negotiation and the kinds of activities that you and your counterpart engage in during the early phases of the negotiation will have a tremendous impact on the results you can produce. Thus, we would recommend that you think about the forms you have filled out and ask yourself before the negotiation: what kinds of issues or information did these forms encourage me to think about? Then, try to have a conversation with your counterpart about the same kinds of issues and information.

For example, the forms in **Chapter 3** dealt with your interests and those of your counterpart. They also pushed you to think about who else might care about the results of the negotiation. In order to be prepared to *negotiate*, you needed to understand your own interests and make some educated guesses about your counterpart's interests. In order to be prepared to *agree*, you and your counterpart need to understand each other's interests, and you need to have explored them sufficiently to uncover the more basic and fundamental things you are each trying to accomplish. Early in your negotiation, you should spend time with your counterpart reviewing your thoughts about who the relevant parties might be and what each of you might care about.

Similarly, the forms in **Chapter 4** dealt with possible options or bits of an agreement. In order to be prepared to negotiate you needed to try to create some possible deals that satisfied each of your interests. The forms in that chapter also encouraged you to be creative and look for ways to collaborate in order to expand the pie. As you prepare to agree, you and your counterpart need to do more of the same: brainstorm possible ways to satisfy each of your interests and possible ways to combine your skills and resources to create more value for both of you.

Not every preparation step lends itself to doing it jointly, however. You need to give some thought to the purpose of each activity. When we discussed walk-away alternatives in **Chapter 5,** for example, we suggested that to be well prepared you should know what you will do if no agreement is reached. Having this information can sometimes help define some limits to the negotiation. If the parties know what each can do if no agreement is reached, then they know that they have to come up with something that is better for each of them than their walk-away alternatives. Yet walking into a negotiation and devoting significant time to discussing what I will do if no agreement is reached may also make my counterpart feel threatened or attacked. If my BATNA is not very good, revealing it might also leave me feeling a little exposed.

The objective criteria and other standards or persuasive processes that you prepared using the forms in **Chapter 6** lend themselves to a frank discussion with the other side. You may or may not want to show them the form you filled out; rather than discuss every possible standard that you thought of, you may want to focus the discussion on those standards that seem persuasive and are relatively favorable to you. But certainly a discussion of possible standards should be an important part of your joint preparation toward an agreement.

In **Chapters 7** and **8,** dealing with communication and relationship, we noted that good communication and relationships do not just happen; they require preparation and effort. Using the forms on your own, and conducting similar kinds of thinking with the other side, you can prepare to agree and to work together to implement whatever your agreement may be.

Finally, a workable commitment will require each of you to agree to do certain things and will require that each of you be satisfied that all the relevant issues have been addressed. Therefore, the process of preparing to agree should include a discussion about the kinds of issues discussed in **Chapter 9.** The forms in that chapter may even serve as a good starting point for joint preparation.

If you have filled out some of the forms in the prior chapters, you have taken an important step toward achieving a better result in your negotiation. Now you should apply the fruits of that effort to help you and your counterpart prepare to agree.

Getting Better at Preparation

We all lead increasingly busy and hectic lives. As we talk to people about the negotiations they carry out at work, at home, and elsewhere, one of the things we hear most often is that they have little enough time to do what they are currently doing, so how can they find additional time to invest in careful and systematic preparation? At the same time, we hear that they often go into important negotiations feeling inadequately or insufficiently prepared.

As we discussed the notion of using tools and forms to get prepared more effectively and more efficiently, we heard a few comments time and again. The first was "That's great. I could really use something to guide me through preparing for a difficult negotiation." The second was "Please include some ideas on how to get better at preparing over time, so that I don't always have to follow the workbook step-by-step." It is to the latter question that we turn now.

Why do people fail to "get better" at preparing for negotiation?

There are many possible causes for the "always too rushed to do it right" feeling when it comes to preparing to negotiate. Our sense is that a few of these have the greatest impact.

We fail to learn from experience

Preparing for negotiation is like any activity that an individual may engage in repeatedly. Experience is the best teacher, yet most people fail to take advantage of it. Every time you negotiate, you have an opportunity to learn something about how well you prepared and how you can continue to get better at preparation. Neglecting that opportunity amounts to turning down some of the best, and least expensive, training available to you.

We fail to practice

Maybe it is because of the time it takes. Perhaps it is for lack of material with which to practice. But the reality is that few negotiators ever make the effort to consider how they might prepare, except when they have a real, live, and probably important negotiation coming up. Consider what that means by imagining a tennis player who played only in tournaments and never practiced, or a musician who put on only concerts or recitals but never rehearsed. When we work on our own cases, in which we are personally and emotionally invested, and when we do so right before having to deal with them, we miss out on all the learning and skill-building afforded by low-risk practice.

We prepare and learn alone

There is a lot we can learn by thinking alone about our experience. We can carefully march through an analysis of our perceptions about how well things worked. But if we fail to involve someone else to serve as a sounding board and coach, to give some sort of reality test to our perceptions, we will forgo learning important lessons that will help us get better faster.

Some bits of advice for getting better

There are a few simple things that you can do, using some of the material in this workbook as well as other resources available to you, that can help you become better over time at preparing to negotiate.

Review

After every negotiation, spend some time reviewing your effort. Your reviews need not take a great deal of time if you structure them to be effective. Our experience is that it is most helpful to start with the successful part. Ask yourself, "What worked?" Put another way, "What are those things you might want to repeat next time you negotiate?" Working backward from the negotiation to the preparation, consider, "What preparation did I do that helped during the nego-tiation?" The answers to these questions should serve as a practical guide to the kinds of preparation habits you want to develop.

Then shift over to those areas where you might improve. Ask yourself, "What would I do differently?" As you think about what you learned from this negotiation that might enable you to do better in the future, consider, "What preparation did I do that was wasted time?" and "What additional preparation would have helped?" If your conclusions from looking at the negotiation are that you would have wanted to do things quite differently, be sure to think about what additional or different preparation you would need to be able to act on these recommendations yourself.

One opportunity to start learning how to review can be found in the pages that follow. We have included for your review a full set of filled-out forms for three of the examples introduced earlier. Whereas in each chapter we included a model for filling out only the two or more forms discussed in that chapter, in this section we have filled out the rest of the forms for each of the chosen ex-amples. Spend a few minutes going through these illustrative preparations. Note how each form adds information not probed for in the prior tool and en-hances the perspective you get of how you might negotiate the case.

Then consider what you might have done differently in analyzing these sit-uations. These filled-out forms are not "answer keys" or perfect models. They are merely illustrations that will give you an opportunity to learn by pushing yourself to see how you would revise them.

Practice

Don't wait until your job, a big deal, or some important relationship is on the line. Look for opportunities to practice your preparation skills. Again, the mate-rials in this workbook should provide you with an easy opportunity to start on your practice. In addition to the three examples for which we included fully filled-out forms, there are three remaining examples from the workbook, for which we have filled out the forms for one element apiece. These are found in the chapters that describe each element. Pick one of these additional cases and work through the remainder of the forms as practice. If these cases do not seem detailed enough, or if you would find it more interesting to work on something more "realistic," pick a situation out of the newspaper or out of your daily experience, which you need not actually negotiate. Put yourself in the shoes of one of the parties and spend some time trying to get ready to negotiate. Use as many of the forms as you think would be appropriate for the case and actually fill them out for practice.

Get help from a colleague

There is no need to go at this alone. Talk to a friend or colleague who might also be interested in learning more about negotiation and about preparing to negotiate. Agree to spend some time helping each other learn from your experiences. It is easier to review and to practice if you do so with someone else who can help you see some of what you may be missing.

An example

Ken is the produce manager at "Saneway," a large supermarket that is part of a national chain. After completing a few management courses offered by his employer, as well as five years of service at the supermarket, he is up for a promotion to assistant store manager. He is about to negotiate his new salary and the terms of his new position.

Ken wants to be promoted to the assistant manager position because it pays more and requires a greater variety of responsibilities. He wants a raise of at least five thousand dollars because: (1) he needs the money; (2) he thinks the job requires more work, responsibility, and headaches, so it should pay more; (3) he's heard a rumor that Wayne, who held this position before relocating to another store, was paid five thousand dollars more than Ken's current salary; and (4) he thinks he deserves it.

Ken is twenty-eight years old and has a bachelor's degree in English literature. He has always had an interest in going back to school and getting a master's degree (although he's not sure what subject to pursue). Money has been an obstacle to a graduate-level education. His only source of funds is what he makes at Saneway, and he really doesn't want and can't afford to take out any more loans. Ken lives in a modest but comfortable studio apartment with his fat cat, Margo. The apartment is at least forty-five minutes away by car from the Saneway store where he is currently working, and there is no easily accessible public transportation. He has recently traded in his beat-up Volkswagen bug for a new Toyota pickup truck.

INTERESTS 1: *Identify the Relevant Parties*

NEGOTIATOR: <u>Ken</u>
COUNTERPART: <u>Lou</u>
SUBJECT: <u>Promotion</u>

Fill in the names of the persons or groups involved in this negotiation. Put yourself as "Negotiator" and the person you are dealing with directly as "Counterpart." In the spaces below, write the names of others who may be significantly affected by the outcome of this negotiation.

People on "my side" who may care about the outcome	People on "their side" who may care about the outcome
Constituents? _____	**Constituents?** Consumers _____
Friends? Jessie, my significant other ____	**Friends?** Colleagues at work _____
Family? _____	**Family?** _____
Boss? _____	**Boss?** Regional director _____
Others? Margo, my cat _____	**Others?** Vendors _____
_____	Saneway Corporation _____

DATE PREPARED: _____   INTERESTS 1

INTERESTS 2: *Clarify the Interests*

NEGOTIATOR: Ken
COUNTERPART: Lou
SUBJECT: Promotion

Mine What do I care about?	**Theirs** If I were in their shoes, what would I care or worry about?	**Others** What are some of the concerns of others who may be significantly affected?

Personal
 Short-term
 1. ~~$5000~~
   not get taken
 2. enough money for rent, cat food and care, car payments, etc.
 3. vacation days
 4. health care
 	
 Long-term
 1. opportunity to grow and advance
 2. go back to school
 	
 Business
 Short-term
 1. promoted to assistant store manager
 2. respect from employer, colleagues, and subordinates
 3. setting a good precedent
 4. incentives and bonuses
 	
 Long-term
 1. maybe get transferred to closer store
 2. be promoted to manager
	Personal
	 1. I look good
	 2. Be perceived as fair
	
	 Business
	 Short-term
	 1. pay lowest salary (what he really cares about is profit)
	 2. need someone flexible/able to adapt to changing environment/policies
	 3. satisfy customers
	 4. assistant store manager needs to:
	  a) make accurate sales projections & salary predictions
	  b) write memos to district managers & department heads
	 Long-term
	 1. relationship with vendors
	 2. profit
	 3. precedent
	 4. groom a loyal & committed employee
		Other 1:
		 Other employees
		 -a good, fair, and consistent manager
		 -good working relationship
		 -don't want Ken to get more than he deserves
		
		 Other 2:
		 Consumers
		 -cheapest prices
		 -fresh produce
		 -quality food
		 -fast & friendly service
		 -store looks nice & clean
		
		 Other 3:
		 Vendors
		 -long-term relationship
		 -access to display space
		 -sell as much as possible at highest price
		 -steady market stream

INTERESTS 3: *Probe for Underlying Interests*

NEGOTIATOR: Ken
COUNTERPART: Lou
SUBJECT: Promotion

In the left-hand column, list the more important interests for you and your counterpart that you identified on the **INTERESTS 2** form. For each of these, ask yourself "why" and "for what purpose?" If you discover deeper interests, list them in the second column. Finally, try to rate your own interests by allocating 100 points among them in proportion to their relative importance.

Important interests (from INTERESTS 2)	Basic or underlying interests (Ask yourself "why?" and "for what purpose?")	Relative importance (Allocate 100 points)
Mine		
Money for living expenses	1. Food, lodging, cat care	30
	2. Fair compensation	10
Promotion to asst. manager	3. Better status	10
	4. Challenge & growth	20
Future opportunities to advance	5. Feel I'm not at a "dead end"	20
Benefits (vacation, health care, etc.)	6. Peace of mind	5
	7. Feel well treated	5
Theirs		
Pay lowest salary possible	1. Profitable store	
Good assistant manager	2. Someone to delegate to	
	3. Accurate sales projections	
	4. Someone to take care of writing memos to headquarters	
	5. Someone flexible	
Happy customers	6. Continued sales	
	7. Good reputation	

DATE PREPARED: _____

OPTIONS 1: *Create Options to Meet Interests*

NEGOTIATOR: Ken
COUNTERPART: Lou
SUBJECT: Promotion

Look at your **INTERESTS 3** form, then list possible ways to meet the interests on both sides. (List interests in order of their relative importance).

My interests	Possible options	Their interests
Money for living expenses	Salary increase	Pay lowest salary possible
	Discount on groceries	
	Incentive pay	
	Service my car at company garage	
Better status	Promotion to asst. manager now, with plan for continued growth	Get a responsible asst. manager to whom Lou can delegate tasks
Future opportunities to advance	Rotation through other departments to get experience	Happy customers
	Opportunity to work with corporate marketing dept	
	Responsibility for dealing with suppliers	
	Assignment to spend time talking to customers to find out what they care most about	

OPTIONS 2: *Find Ways to Maximize Joint Gains*

NEGOTIATOR: Ken

COUNTERPART: Lou

SUBJECT: Promotion

Consider ways to combine skills and resources to satisfy key interests on both sides.

	Inventory of skills and resources	Combine similar resources to produce value	Combine different resources to produce value

Me	Management skills
	
	Dedication
	
	Enthusiasm
	
	5 years' experience
	
	Writing ability
		Work on a plan to increase customer satisfaction and make store a showcase
		
		Work on plan to have me help train new staff
			Develop a training and advancement plan for me that keeps me productive and growing
			
			Put my writing skills to work for Saneway:
			  -marketing
			  -new training materials
			
			Give me more benefits & less pay, so better for me and cheaper for Saneway

Them	Money Training programs Advancement opportunities Dedication to customer service Purchasing power for benefits		

ALTERNATIVES 1: *Think of My Alternatives to a Negotiated Agreement*

My key interests

1. $ to cover needs
2. Promotion to asst. store manager
3. Opportunity for growth
4. Incentives, bonuses, benefits

What could I do to satisfy my interests if we do not reach an agreement?

Possible alternatives	Pros	Cons
1. Quit and work at another store	Easy to do with my experience; may start at higher salary?	Some risk; lose seniority; lose working relationships built up over 5 years
2. Continue as produce manager and tighten my budget	No risk, easy to do	$ tight; lose respect of my co-workers for wimping out?
3. Look for other positions within Saneway	Keep seniority I've built up; stay with company I know; may get on a faster track	Don't know if there are other positions
4. Go back to school	Interesting; helps growth	Expensive; more loans!

ALTERNATIVES 2: *Select and Improve My BATNA*

Of my alternatives, what will I really do if no agreement is reached (my BATNA)? Why?

   #3: Look for other positions within Saneway; combines opportunity for growth with lower risk.

What can I do to improve my BATNA? (Write down concrete steps you could take to improve your BATNA even before you go into the negotiation.)

   Ask Personnel Dept. about positions that I would be interested in/qualified for and likelihood of their opening up.

ALTERNATIVES 3: *Identify Alternatives Open to the Other Side*

NEGOTIATOR: Ken
COUNTERPART: Lou
SUBJECT: Promotion

Their key interests:

1. Pay lowest salary possible
2. Find good asst. store manager
3. Satisfy customers
4. Be perceived as fair

What could they do to satisfy their interests if we do not reach an agreement?

Alternatives	Pros	Cons
1. Look for someone else to promote	May not have to pay them as much	Have to fill in job himself until gets someone else; have to waste time interviewing people, etc.
2. Hire temp until get full-time asst. manager	Solves immediate need	Have to train the temp, then train the full-time person
3. Shift responsibilities around and eliminate asst. manager position	Saves money; look like a hero	Tough to do; more work for Lou; may get resistance from others

ALTERNATIVES 4: *Estimate Their BATNA*

What would I do in their shoes? (Which of their self-help alternatives looks best for them?)

#3: Shift responsibilities and eliminate position

How might I legitimately make their BATNA less attractive?

By making it harder to pursue ?	By influencing their perception of how unwise or costly it might be?
Explain to colleagues how important the asst. manager position is and how it helps them do their jobs (so that they'll resist eliminating it)	Remind Lou of everything Wayne did to make things function smoothly

LEGITIMACY 1: *Use External Standards as a Sword and as a Shield*

What specific substantive question has to be answered in this negotiation?

What should my salary be if I get the promotion?

Possible standards (precedents, benchmarks, prior practice, accepted principles, etc.)

Place each standard along a range from least favorable to you, to most favorable to you. Below each standard, indicate what that standard would mean in this case.

	Standards:	Current salary	Wayne's salary for asst. mgr.	Wayne's old salary + inflation	Wayne's new salary at new store	
Least favorable ←	Application of standard to this case:	$18,000	$23,000	$24,000	$27,000	→ **Most favorable**

Other standards that may be relevant or that require research:

Salaries of assistant managers at other stores:
    —other Saneway stores
    —competitors

Persuasive processes

If you cannot agree on an answer, you might agree on the process to find an agreeable answer. If one of the following looks interesting, how might you apply it to this case?

"I cut, you choose"

Flip a coin

Get an expert opinion

    Ask an employment service what the going rate would be

Let an arbitrator decide

The test of reciprocity

In some cases, reciprocity can be very persuasive. Are there some negotiations in which your counterpart is in a position similar to yours?

    Yes, when negotiating his own salary

If so, what standards or arguments does he or she use in the situation?

    Probably the value of his experience

How could you apply those standards or arguments here?

    Focus on what I've learned and accomplished in 5 years

If they had to explain the result of this negotiation to someone important to them, they could convince their constituents with the following few points:

1. "It's a fair deal based on Ken's experience and the previous salaries that have been paid for this position."

2. "I'm not paying any more than we were paying and I'm getting an eager and enthusiastic employee with experience and training."

3.

4.

COMMUNICATION 1: *Question My Assumptions and Identify Things to Listen For*

NEGOTIATOR: Ken

COUNTERPART: Lou

SUBJECT: Promotion

The first step in dealing with your blind spots is to become aware of them. In the left-hand column, list your assumptions about their intentions and perceptions. In the right-hand column, write down key phrases your counterpart might say that should lead you to question your assumptions.

My assumptions (I assume that . . .)	Things to listen for
Lou won't want to give me the position.	Lou says, "I'm pleased that you are interested in the position."
Lou won't want to give me the raise I want.	Lou says, "I want to be fair about salary."
Lou doesn't think I have enough experience for the job.	Lou says, "You've been working here quite some time, and I know you are a qualified candidate."
Lou thinks I am perfect for the job.	Lou doesn't look me in the eye and hesitates when talking about me and the job.

COMMUNICATION 2: *Reframe to Help Them Understand*

NEGOTIATOR: Ken

COUNTERPART: Lou

SUBJECT: Promotion

Your perspective	How might they hear it?	Reframing
(List 3–5 statements you might make to clearly put forth your interests.)	(For each statement, list your counterpart's possible response, e.g., "Yes, but ...")	(Restate your interests so that they will hear them better.)
1. I would like a $5,000 raise.	You want a huge jump in salary.	I want to be fairly compensated for the work I do and for the responsibilities I take on.
2. I deserve the job and salary I'm asking for.	You've been a steady worker, but no one is "entitled" to a promotion.	I believe my recent training and experience make me a good candidate.
3. I want to be on a track for advancement.	Is Ken after _my_ job?	I'd like your help in developing a plan that keeps me growing and contributing.

RELATIONSHIP 1: *Separate People Issues from Substantive Issues*

NEGOTIATOR: Ken

COUNTERPART: Lou

SUBJECT: Promotion

Describe your relationship (Use adjectives.)

Friendly but with some distance

Separate the relationship from the substance

Substantive issues and problems	Relationship issues and problems
(money, terms, dates, and conditions)	(reliability, mutual acceptance, emotions, etc.)
Salary increase	Fair treatment
Responsibilities	Reliable information (*e.g., about what Wayne or others make*)

Substantive options and remedies	Ways to improve the relationship
(Consider referring to the chapters on **Interests** and **Options**)	(Make sure these are not substantive concessions)
Better benefits (health package, vacation time)	Use objective standards
Paying for education	Ask Personnel Dept. for data on average salaries for certain roles
Extra training	

RELATIONSHIP 2: *Prepare to Build a Good Working Relationship*

NEGOTIATOR: Ken
COUNTERPART: Lou
SUBJECT: Promotion

What might be wrong now?	What can *I* do . . .
What might be causing any present misunderstanding?	**. . . to try to understand them better?**
Rumor mill	Speak directly and set aside gossip
What might be causing a lack of trust?	**. . . to demonstrate my reliability?**
Lack of reliable information	Don't make assertions or claims about things I don't know
What might be causing one or both of us to feel coerced?	**. . . to put the focus on persuasion instead of coercion?**
Lou's need to get the role filled	Offer to start filling in on some asst. manager tasks for a week, while we work things out
What might be causing one or both of us to feel disrespected?	**. . . to show acceptance and respect?**
What might be causing one or both of us to get upset?	**. . . to balance emotion and reason?**

COMMITMENT 1: *Identify the Issues to Be Included in the Agreement*

NEGOTIATOR: Ken

COUNTERPART: Lou

SUBJECT: Promotion

Overall purpose of negotiation

Discuss promotion and salary opportunity

Expected product of negotiation

(Draft a table of contents for a final agreement that would be operational and durable.)

Job responsibilities
Salary
Training plan
Start date
Schedule

Specific purpose of next meeting

Review specific training for position

Tangible product of next meeting

(If you could imagine the piece of paper you would produce during *this* meeting, what would it contain?)

____ A list of options for further consideration?

____ An action plan for further work necessary before an agreement would be possible?

____ A joint recommendation to your respective organizations?

____ An agreement in principle?

____ A signed contract?

✓ Commitments toward the next steps?

____ Other _____

COMMITMENT 2: *Plan the Steps to Agreement*

NEGOTIATOR: Ken
COUNTERPART: Lou
SUBJECT: Promotion

Decision makers: names of those who will "sign" the agreement

Lou and I

Implementation: information that the agreement should include about what happens next

Implementors who should perhaps be consulted before agreement is final:

Key co-workers?

Possible obstacles to implementation:

Resistance by someone else who wants the job?
Corporate regulations on requirements for the position?

Ways to deal with obstacles:

Consult Personnel Dept. Be clear about my qualifications for the position

Steps necessary to get to a binding agreement

	Target date
1. Tentative agreement on issues to be included:	Done
2. Clarification of interests on each issue:	First meeting: tomorrow
3. Discussion of options for handling each issue:	Tomorrow
4. My draft of a framework agreement:	End of the week?
5. Joint working draft of possible agreement:	
6. Final text ready for signature:	Two weeks

An example

Liz is a regional manager with Wholesale Foods, a large and growing national produce distributor. She is responsible for managing relationships with suppliers, mostly small farmers in the state, as well as customers of Wholesale Foods, who range from small corner grocers to the stores of the largest regional supermarket chain. One of the suppliers with whom she must negotiate is Terry, the owner of a small fruit orchard at the northeast corner of the state.

As the manager of a large territory, Liz has to worry about her profitability, which in turn is a function of the price at which she buys and sells produce. But her profitability is also affected by the amount of effort it takes her to get the produce to market and how much she has to spend to overcome glitches in her delivery system. For example, if a farmer is late with his deliveries, Liz has to spend money to get produce from somewhere else, usually at a higher price, to meet her obligations to her customers; or if a farmer delivers fruit in bulk, Liz has to spend money to crate it properly. Similarly, her profitability is related to the price she can get for the produce from her customers. If she can develop a reputation for being a source of "quality" produce, she can get an extra few cents per pound over average market prices, which rapidly adds up to big profits. To manage some of these risks, Liz maintains a small fleet of closed-bed trucks capable of traveling around the state and employs a few more workers than is absolutely necessary in her warehouses.

Terry is his own boss, running a farm that has been in his family for three generations. Over his lifetime he has seen the farm experiment with a number of different crops, but at significant risk: a bad harvest with a supposedly improved strain of one of his traditional crops could wipe him out. Similarly, the risk of planting something different and not being able to sell it at a good price could mean not being able to pay off the season's debts at harvest time, which in turn would mean not being able to buy needed stocks and supplies at planting time. Terry has one open-bed pickup truck he uses to bring in supplies and deliver fruit. He hires only seasonal help, at planting and harvest times.

Each year, Liz and Terry get together and discuss terms: quantities and prices for his fruit, the dates on which delivery should be made, how the fruit will be crated, etc. Although they get along, Liz has the sense that there is more they could do that would be mutually profitable.

INTERESTS 1: *Identify the Relevant Parties*

Fill in the names of the persons or groups involved in this negotiation. Put yourself as "Negotiator" and the person you are dealing with directly as "Counterpart." In the spaces below, write the names of others who may be significantly affected by the outcome of this negotiation.

People on "my side" who may care about the outcome	People on "their side" who may care about the outcome
Constituents? Wholesale Foods employees	**Constituents?** Farm employees
Friends? _____	**Friends?** Neighboring farmers
Family? _____	**Family?** Terry's family
Boss? V.P. Operations	**Boss?** _____
Others? Customers	**Others?** _____
Other suppliers	

INTERESTS 2: *Clarify the Interests*

Mine What do I care about?	**Theirs** If I were in their shoes, what would I care or worry about?	**Others** What are the concerns of others who may be significantly affected?
Personal	**Personal**	**Other 1:** Customers
Look good to boss	Keep family fed/happy	Quality produce
Continue good working relationship		Delivery on time
		Good price
		Other 2: Other suppliers
		Fair treatment
		Good terms for their produce
Business	**Business**	
Good reputation for quality produce	Good price on crops	
Profit from: buying and selling quality produce	Farm survival	
	Good harvests	
	Low-risk crops	**Other 3:**
efficient time spent on getting produce to market	Staying out of debt—low overhead	
No delivery glitches	Having enough stocks/supplies for planting	
Properly crated produce	Fair deal with buyers	

INTERESTS 3: *Probe for Underlying Interests*

NEGOTIATOR: Liz
COUNTERPART: Terry
SUBJECT: Fruit deal

In the left-hand column, list the more important interests for you and your counterpart that you identified on the **INTERESTS 2** form. For each of these, ask yourself "why?" and "for what purpose?" If you discover deeper interests, list them in the second column. Finally, try to rate your own interests by allocating 100 points among them in proportion to their relative importance.

Important interests (from INTERESTS 2)	Basic or underlying interests (Ask yourself "why?" and "for what purpose?")	Relative importance (Allocate 100 points)
Mine		
Good reputation for quality produce	Bring in more business Keep customers happy	40
Make profit	Look good to boss Earn a bonus Good for the company	40
Smooth delivery	Free up time for other things Keep customers happy Fewer hassles = more profitable business	20
Theirs		
Keep family fed/happy	Same	
Good price for crops	Meet minimum financial needs Make a profit Develop cushion for hard times	
Low-risk crops	Avoid disaster Not put family at risk Predictable harvest and market	

OPTIONS 1: *Create Options to Meet Interests*

NEGOTIATOR: Liz

COUNTERPART: Terry

SUBJECT: Fruit deal

Look at your **INTERESTS 3** form, then list possible ways to meet the interests on both sides. (List interests in order of their relative importance).

My interests	Possible options	Their interests
1. Revenue	Pay premium price for premium quality	1. Revenue
2. Quality	Pay bonus for on-time delivery	2. Quality
3. Reliability	Share cost of crating	3. Reliability
4. Crating	Advance cash at planting time, to risk on new products	4. Crating
5. Competitive advantage over other wholesalers	Exclusive deal in exchange for guaranteed contract to buy all that Terry produces that meets minimum quality standard	5. Quick and effective harvest
6. Access to other products		6. Liquidity during planting
7. Brand image		7. Shipping insurance

OPTIONS 2: *Find Ways to Maximize Joint Gains*

Consider ways to combine skills and resources to satisfy key interests on both sides.

	Inventory of skills and resources	Combine similar resources to produce value	Combine different resources to produce value
Me	Money Closed-bed trucks Steady labor Customers/market Market savvy	1. We might pool our trucks and use each for what it's best suited. 2. We might pool our purchases to get a better price (fuel, tires, spare parts)	1. I could provide extra labor at harvest time to help pack produce in smaller crates. 2. We could work together to identify specialty produce he could grow and I could finance and market. 3. We could put labels on the best fruit to create a positive brand image. 4. I could advance Terry some payment at planting time.
Them	Produce Land Seasonal labor Farming experience Open-bed trucks Opportunity to recognize and separate the "best" fruit		

ALTERNATIVES 1: *Think of My Alternatives to a Negotiated Agreement*

NEGOTIATOR: Liz

COUNTERPART: Terry

SUBJECT: Fruit deal

My key interests

1. Good reputation for quality produce
2. Make profit
3. Smooth delivery
4. Properly crated produce

What could I do to satisfy my interests if we do not reach an agreement?

Possible alternatives	Pros	Cons
1. Find another fruit farmer	Shouldn't be too hard May be able to insist on better quality and price terms from the start	Have to start over with someone I don't know
2. Start a farm, owned by our company	We'd have more control over what is planted and over costs	Tough business to get into Lots of time and effort required
3. Stop offering certain produce (Terry's) to my customers	Easy to do	Lose profit potential Annoy customers Hurt reputation

Of my alternatives, what will I really do if no agreement is reached (my BATNA)? Why?

#1. Find another fruit farmer—it's the least risky alternative.

What can I do to improve my BATNA? (Write down concrete steps you could take to improve your BATNA even before you go into the negotiation.)

Call other suppliers now, so I know what's available.
Talk to buyers about other local farms.

ALTERNATIVES 3: *Identify Alternatives Open to the Other Side*

NEGOTIATOR: Liz

COUNTERPART: Terry

SUBJECT: Fruit deal

Their key interests:

1. Keep family fed/happy
2. Good price on crops
3. Good harvest
4. Fair deal
5. Low risk/low debt

What could they do to satisfy their interests if we do not reach an agreement?

Alternatives	Pros	Cons
1. Find another wholesaler to buy his crops.	Diversifies his client base. Helps him sell more produce. May get better terms.	Takes time to find another wholesaler. Business is tight; it's not easy to find new customers. Would have to deal with someone he doesn't know well.
2. Sell the farm.	Get out of business with lots of ups and downs.	Give up family tradition. What else does he know how to do?

ALTERNATIVES 4: *Estimate Their BATNA*

What would I do in their shoes? (Which of their self-help alternatives looks best for them?)

#1. Find another wholesaler

How might I legitimately make their BATNA less attractive?

By making it harder to pursue?	By influencing their perception of how unwise or costly it might be?
Complain a little to other wholesalers I know about how expensive Terry has gotten?	Show Terry some articles about how tough the wholesale produce business has become.

NEGOTIATOR: Liz

COUNTERPART: Terry

SUBJECT: Fruit deal

What specific substantive question has to be answered in this negotiation?

Price for his produce (e.g., strawberries)

Possible standards (precedents, benchmarks, prior practice, accepted principles, etc.)

Place each standard along a range from least favorable to you, to most favorable to you. Below each standard indicate what that standard would mean in this case.

	Standards:	Roadside farmstand price	Last year's price + quality bonus	Last year's price + inflation	Last year's price	Cost of planting + harvesting	
Least favorable	Application of standard to this case:	33¢/pt	20¢	17¢	16¢	12¢	Most favorable

Other standards that may be relevant or that require research:

Price at neighboring farms

Additional margin over cost, which Terry needs to cover occasional bad harvest

Price at which we sell to grocery stores

DATE PREPARED: ———————————

Persuasive processes

If you cannot agree on an answer, you might agree on the process to find an agreeable answer. If one of the following looks interesting, how might you apply it to this case?

"I cut, you choose"

Tell Terry we can pick up and crate for ___ cents per pound and let him choose how to deliver.

Flip a coin

Get an expert opinion

Get county fair judge to say how much better than average (or not) Terry's fruit is.

Let an arbitrator decide

The test of reciprocity

In some cases, reciprocity can be very persuasive. Are there some negotiations in which your counterpart is in a position similar to yours?

Terry buys from seed and supply vendors.

If so, what standards or arguments does he or she use in the situation?

He probably asks for a discount for being long-term customer.

How could you apply those standards or arguments here?

Ask for a discount for guaranteeing that we'll buy his harvest, year in and year out.

LEGITIMACY 3: *Offer Them an Attractive Way to Explain Their Decision*

If they had to explain the result of this negotiation to someone important to them, they could convince their constituents with the following few points:

1. "It's a fair deal compared to other farmers."

2. "It allows us some room to experiment and maybe make more money later."

3. "It's no different than what I would ask of my suppliers."

4.

COMMUNICATION 1: *Question My Assumptions and Identify Things to Listen For*

NEGOTIATOR: Liz

COUNTERPART: Terry

SUBJECT: Fruit deal

The first step in dealing with your blind spots is to become aware of them. In the left-hand column, list your assumptions about their intentions and perceptions. In the right-hand column, write down key phrases your counterpart might say that should lead you to question your assumptions.

My assumptions (I assume that . . .)	Things to listen for
He may resist spending more time on this negotiation.	Do you have some new ideas?
He won't want to try something different.	I've been reading about some new equipment and techniques.
He's committed to hiring his part-time laborers at harvest time.	It's getting harder and harder to find good people at a reasonable wage.

COMMUNICATION 2: *Reframe to Help Them Understand*

NEGOTIATOR: Liz
COUNTERPART: Terry
SUBJECT: Fruit deal

Your perspective	How might they hear it?	Reframing
(List 3–5 statements you might make to clearly put forth your interests.)	(For each statement, list your counterpart's possible response, e.g., "Yes, but . . .")	(Restate your interests so that way they will hear them better.)
I need the fruit properly crated.	You're asking me to do something I can't do.	How can we work together to ensure speedy delivery to market that won't impose an undue burden on either of us?
I need assurances that you will deliver on time.	I give you my word, I'll do the best I can do.	Let's brainstorm together what we can do to ensure on-time delivery and what to do if it doesn't happen.
I want to label your best fruit as "premium" brand.	She wants to pay me less for the other fruit? She wants to make more work for me.	I wonder how we might be able to separate out the best fruit and charge more money for it.

RELATIONSHIP 1: *Separate People Issues from Substantive Issues*

NEGOTIATOR: Liz

COUNTERPART: Terry

SUBJECT: Fruit deal

Describe your relationship. (Use adjectives.)

Businesslike; collaborative

Separate the relationship from the substance

Substantive issues and problems	Relationship issues and problems
(money, terms, dates, and conditions)	(reliability, mutual acceptance, emotions, etc.)
Price per pound	It is good
Delivery dates	
Crating procedures	
Payment plan	
Amount of fruit	

Substantive options and remedies	Ways to improve the relationship
(Consider referring to the chapters on **Interests** and **Options**)	(Make sure these are not substantive concessions)
Research other wholesale fruit prices	Keep doing what we are doing
Contingency plan for ensuring follow-through	-listening to each other
	-consulting first
	-presenting solutions instead of problems

DATE PREPARED: _____

RELATIONSHIP 2: *Prepare to Build a Good Working Relationship*

NEGOTIATOR: Liz
COUNTERPART: Terry
SUBJECT: Fruit deal

What might be wrong now?	What can *I* do . . .
What might be causing any present mis-understanding?	**. . . to try to understand them better?**
History of not exploring interests	Ask questions; work to put myself in his shoes.
What might be causing a lack of trust?	**. . . to demonstrate my reliability?**
Perceptions about differences between urban and rural lifestyles	Come out to see him; dress in jeans.
What might be causing one or both of us to feel coerced?	**. . . to put the focus on persuasion instead of coercion?**
What might be causing one or both of us to feel disrespected?	**. . . to show acceptance and respect?**
What might be causing one or both of us to get upset?	**. . . to balance emotion and reason?**
We haven't; but we could. It would be out of fear of ending up with no deal at the last minute	Know my BATNA, so I can keep my cool. Don't push him on his BATNA too hard or too soon.

DATE PREPARED: _____

Overall purpose of negotiation

Discuss and decide terms of deal

Expected product of negotiation

(Draft a table of contents for a final agreement that would be operational and durable.)

Quantities of fruit
Prices of Fruit
Delivery dates
Payment plan
Contingency plan
Penalty clauses

Specific purpose of next meeting

Explore possible ways to improve existing deal

Tangible product of next meeting

(If you could imagine the piece of paper you would produce during *this* meeting, what would it contain?)

✓ A list of options for further consideration?
___ An action plan for further work necessary before an agreement would be possible?
___ A joint recommendation to your respective organizations?
___ An agreement in principle?
___ A signed contract?
___ Commitments toward the next steps?
___ Other _____

COMMITMENT 2: *Plan the Steps to Agreement*

NEGOTIATOR: Liz
COUNTERPART: Terry
SUBJECT: Fruit deal

Decision makers: names of those who will "sign" the agreement

Terry and Liz

Implementation: information that the agreement should include about what happens next

Implementors who should perhaps be consulted before agreement is final:

My trucking & warehousing people?

Possible obstacles to implementation:

Weather: sickness in Terry's family; his truck breaking down

Ways to deal with obstacles:

Contingency plans & good communication

Steps necessary to get to a binding agreement	Target date
1. Tentative agreement on issues to be included:	Next meeting (Tuesday)
2. Clarification of interests on each issue:	Same
3. Discussion of options for handling each issue:	Same
4. My draft of a framework agreement:	A week later
5. Joint working draft of possible agreement:	End of the month

An example

KidWorld Mfg. Co. and the Assembly Workers of America have been negotiating a new three-year contract for weeks. They have successfully resolved a number of issues, reaching tentative agreements on wages, work rules, and performance bonuses. The next issue for discussion, however, promises to be a difficult one.

Health care has become a very sensitive issue around KidWorld. As part of its benefits package for assembly-line workers, KidWorld absorbs approximately 50 percent of workers' health-related costs. This percentage takes into account insurance premiums, co-payments, deductibles, etc. A study done by outside consultants suggested that KidWorld's current health care–related expenses added 12 percent to the cost of every toy sold, a figure approximately 4 times greater than its overseas competitors. The board is also concerned that health care expenses have increased faster than any cost other than employee wages, which, including performance bonuses, have grown at twice the inflation rate.

The union is also concerned about health care. They have polled their workers and found that the declining purchasing power of their health care dollars ranks second in employee concern preceded only by fears about the security of their pensions. Over the last few years, the company's insurance coverage has failed to keep up with inflation in the health sector, and employee contributions and co-payments have both increased. KidWorld ranks in the top half of employers organized by the Assembly Workers of America in terms of health care benefits but below a significant number of companies similar in size and structure, of its domestic competitors.

The union's negotiating team is preparing to meet with their company counterpart. Traditionally, this issue has been a difficult one to negotiate. The union team has come in asking for the moon (typically full coverage of any and all health-related costs), and the company has come in complaining about how rising health-care costs are making it lose ground to foreign competition. In the last few negotiations, the company has started by seeking to get the union to "give back" some health benefits.

This year, the union has decided to go into the negotiations with something more than bluster and the threat of labor trouble. In addition to thinking hard about possible creative solutions to the problem posed by rising health-care costs, they will also try to bring to the table persuasive standards for dealing with the issue.

INTERESTS 1: *Identify the Relevant Parties*

NEGOTIATOR: Union team

COUNTERPART: KidWorld team

SUBJECT: Health care benefits

Fill in the names of the persons or groups involved in this negotiation. Put yourself as "Negotiator" and the person you are dealing with directly as "Counterpart." In the spaces below, write the names of others who may be significantly affected by the outcome of this negotiation.

People on "my side" who may care about the outcome	People on "their side" who may care about the outcome
Constituents? Rank & file union members	**Constituents?** Management
Friends?	**Friends?**
Family? Yes!	**Family?**
Boss? Union president	**Boss?** CEO
Others? Non-union KidWorld employees	**Others?** Non-union KidWorld employees Other toy companies Customers

INTERESTS 2: *Clarify the Interests*

Mine What do I care about?	**Theirs** If I were in their shoes, what would I care or worry about?	**Others** What are the concerns of others who may be significantly affected?
Personal Efficient, easy negotiation Ability to explain results	**Personal** Look good to boss Efficient, easy negotiation Ability to explain results	**Other 1:** CEO Profitability of company **Other 2:** Customers Good quality products Good service Competitive prices
Business Good health care package Low costs to employees Fair treatment Voice in decision making that affects us Good morale among employees Decrease employee contributions	**Business** Keep costs down Able to compete with other mfg. cos. Set good precedent Finish negotiations, without strike	**Other 3:** Other KidWorld employees Fairness for their benefits

INTERESTS 3: *Probe for Underlying Interests*

NEGOTIATOR: Union team
COUNTERPART: KidWorld team
SUBJECT: Health care benefits

In the left-hand column, list the more important interests for you and your counterpart that you identified on the **INTERESTS 2** form. For each of these, ask yourself "why?" and "for what purpose?" If you discover deeper interests, list them in the second column. Finally, try to rate your own interests by allocating 100 points among them in proportion to their relative importance.

Important interests (from **INTERESTS 2**)	Basic or underlying interests (Ask yourself "why?" and "for what purpose?")	Relative importance (Allocate 100 points)
Mine		
Voice in decision making	Have a say in how our money is used Feeling more a part of the company Being taken seriously	30
Good health care package	Access to good medical care Fair treatment	35
Decrease employee contribution	Free up disposable income for other things (vacation, etc.)	35
Theirs		
Look good to boss	Career advancement—get more responsibility	
Keep costs down	Be competitive in the market Improve price of company stock	
Good precedent	Make it easier in the future, with us and other unions	
Avoid strike	Minimize disruption Avoid cost of strike	

OPTIONS 1: *Create Options to Meet Interests*

Look at your **INTERESTS 3** form, then list possible ways to meet the interests on both sides. (List interests in order of their relative importance).

My interests	Possible options	Their interests
Having a say in how our money is spent	Involve union in process of selecting and evaluating	Good precedent
Good health care package	Insurance plans	Keep costs down
	Create preventive health programs to reduce overall cost	
Feel part of the company	Create joint union/management committees to work through specific health care issues	Avoid strike
Be taken seriously		
Free up disposable income for other things	Design escalator clauses in case costs increase and develop incentives to keep costs down	Be competitive Improve stock price

DATE PREPARED: _____   OPTIONS 1

OPTIONS 2: *Find Ways to Maximize Joint Gains*

Consider ways to combine skills and resources to satisfy key interests on both sides.

	Inventory of skills and resources	Combine similar resources to produce value	Combine different resources to produce value
Me	Ability to mobilize and motivate union members Ability to evaluate plans	Joint evaluation plans Joint design of ideal plan, to get bids on it Ability to promote collaboration Ability to serve as "model client" for some progressive health care provider	Trade off some sick days for smaller deductibles? Set up and promote preventive health program to decrease medical problems and costs (exercise, blood pressure monitoring, etc.) Give union opportunity to find a better deal to save cost to the company
Them	$$ Space in factories Ability to evaluate plans		

ALTERNATIVES 1: *Think of My Alternatives to a Negotiated Agreement*

My key interests

1. Voice in decisions
2. Good health care coverage
3. Low-cost employee contribution
4. Fair treatment

What could I do to satisfy my interests if we do not reach an agreement?

Possible alternatives	Pros	Cons
1. Strike	Easy to call Can probably get the votes	Bad for everyone
2. Union buys supplementary coverage	We get exactly what we want	Expensive? Difficult to administer
3. Lobby Congress for universal coverage	Would shift burden to employer Can get other unions to help	Long-term solution, not for this year Expensive effort May not succeed

ALTERNATIVES 2: *Select and Improve My BATNA*

Of my alternatives, what will I really do if no agreement is reached (my BATNA)? Why?

#2: Union-sponsored supplemental coverage. This would solve members' needs and let us choose how to spend our money.

What can I do to improve my BATNA? (Write down concrete steps you could take to improve your BATNA even before you go into the negotiation.)

Contact a few insurers to get some proposals.

ALTERNATIVES 3: *Identify Alternatives Open to the Other Side*

NEGOTIATOR: Union team
COUNTERPART: KidWorld team
SUBJECT: Health care benefits

Their key interests:

1. Good precedent
2. Be competitive with other toy companies
3. Keep costs down
4. Avoid strike

What could they do to satisfy their interests if we do not reach an agreement?

Alternatives	Pros	Cons
1. Try to impose terms	Easy to try	Might cause a strike
2. Try to go around us— directly to membership	Puts pressure on us May get them a better deal May make us look bad	Bad for long-term relationship with union We could fight back
3. Take the case to arbitration	Avoids strike	Costly Uncertain result

ALTERNATIVES 4: *Estimate Their BATNA*

What would I do in their shoes? (Which of their self-help alternatives looks best for them?)

#3. Take the case to arbitration

How might I legitimately make their BATNA less attractive?

By making it harder to pursue ?	By influencing their perception of how unwise or costly it might be?
Prepare arguments on why this issue shouldn't be a subject for arbitration	Get information from our lawyer about what we could argue in arbitration

What specific substantive question has to be answered in this negotiation?

How much of total cost should company pay?

Possible standards (precedents, benchmarks, prior practice, accepted principles, etc.)

Place each standard along a range from least favorable to you, to most favorable to you. Below each standard, indicate what that standard would mean in this case.

	Foreign competitors	Peer mfg. co.	KidWorld Current level	U.S. toy cos.	KidHaven Stores	?	
Least favorable ← Standards: Application of standard to this case:	25%	40%	50%	65%	75%	100%	→ **Most favorable**

Other standards that may be relevant or that require research:

Inflation = 3%/yr   Health care inflation = 12%/yr
Salaried workers at KidWorld = ?
Pension plan matching contribution = 100%
Percentage of total wages employees must devote to health care = ?
Compared to: Salaried workers? Foreign competitors? KidHaven Stores?

LEGITIMACY 2: *Use the Fairness of the Process to Persuade*

NEGOTIATOR: Union team

COUNTERPART: KidWorld team

SUBJECT: Health care benefits

Persuasive processes

If you cannot agree on an answer, you might agree on the process to find an agreeable answer. If one of the following looks interesting, how might you apply it to this case?

"I cut, you choose"

Flip a coin

Get an expert opinion

Let an arbitrator decide   Final offer arbitration?   (As in baseball, arbitrator chooses between each side's final offer.)

Most-favored nation   Agree on a number, but if KidWorld gives anyone else a better deal, we get it too.

The test of reciprocity

In some cases, reciprocity can be very persuasive. Are there some negotiations in which your counterpart is in a position similar to yours?

Yes, when negotiating with retailers about co-op advertising.

If so, what standards or arguments does he or she use in the situation?

KidWorld wants a say in how their money is used and an opportunity to get a better deal.

How could you apply those standards or arguments here?

We might say the same things: the union should have a say in how employee contributions are used, and an opportunity to shop around.

LEGITIMACY 3: *Offer Them an Attractive Way to Explain Their Decision*

If they had to explain the result of this negotiation to someone important to them, they could convince their constituents with the following few points:

1. "This is in line with other benefits at KidWorld and with industry practice."

2. "We're holding the line at a level that keeps us competitive."

3. "It's only fair to give employees a chance to participate in deciding how health care dollars are spent for their own benefit. We want the same thing when retailers spend our money on advertising."

4.

COMMUNICATION 1: *Question My Assumptions and Identify Things to Listen For*

NEGOTIATOR: Union team
COUNTERPART: KidWorld team
SUBJECT: Health care benefits

The first step in dealing with your blind spots is to become aware of them. In the left-hand column, list your assumptions about their intentions and perceptions. In the right-hand column, write down key phrases your counterpart might say that should lead you to question your assumptions.

My assumptions (I assume that . . .)	Things to listen for
They want to force us to pay more for health care and lower their contributions.	We want this deal to be acceptable to the employees.
	We want to work with you to get the best coverage possible at a price that keeps us competitive in the market.
They want to get their way.	Tell us what's important to you. How might we do this together?
They only care about looking good.	Let's consider a broad range of options, without worrying too much now about whether they'd be practical.

COMMUNICATION 2: *Reframe to Help Them Understand*

Your perspective (List 3–5 statements you might make to clearly put forth your interests.)	How might they hear it? (For each statement, list your counterpart's possible response, e.g., "Yes, but . . .")	Reframing (Restate your interests so that they will hear them better.)
You want us to pay too much.	We're already contributing more than many companies.	How can we build a plan that allows us to compete but also feels fair to the employees?
We demand good quality health care.	We can't afford to buy each of you a Cadillac either!	We care and we want you to care about the quality of the medical benefits we and our families receive.
We want a voice in the decision making.	They'll always pick the most expensive plan and insist on it.	If we could participate in the process of choosing health plans, we might understand the trade-offs more clearly and feel better about how our money is spent.

RELATIONSHIP 1: *Separate People Issues from Substantive Issues*

Describe your relationship (Use adjectives.)

Adversarial, hostile, distrustful

Separate the relationship from the substance

Substantive issues and problems (money, terms, dates, and conditions)	**Relationship issues and problems** (reliability, mutual acceptance, emotions, etc.)
Cost to employees	Not listening
Date of implementation	Name calling
Inflation for health care	Thinking each other is unreasonable
Frequency of payments by employees	
Amount of coverage	
Deductible	

Substantive options and remedies (Consider referring to the chapters on **Interests** and **Options**)	**Ways to improve the relationship** (Make sure these are not substantive concessions)
Use market standards for employee contribution	Let other side express concerns first
Allow union to participate in choice of plans	Try to put self in other side's shoes
Offer multiple options to employees	Promise not to call each other names—seek similar commitment from other side
Set up preventive health program	

RELATIONSHIP 2: *Prepare to Build a Good Working Relationship*

What might be wrong now?	What can *I* do . . .
What might be causing any present mis-understanding	**. . . to try to understand them better?**
Prior history Difficult terminology	Spend time clarifying perceptions, before tackling the substance.
What might be causing a lack of trust?	**. . . to demonstrate my reliability?**
What might be causing one or both of us to feel coerced?	**. . . to put the focus on persuasion instead of coercion?**
The possibility of a strike	Consider ways to resolve this without a strike. Agree to let panel of experts decide?
What might be causing one or both of us to feel disrespected?	**. . . to show acceptance and respect?**
Strong language used in the past	Have a kick-off dinner before the negotiations? Agree that whatever happens we'll treat each other with respect.
What might be causing one or both of us to get upset?	**. . . to balance emotion and reason?**

COMMITMENT 1: *Identify the Issues to Be Included in the Agreement*

Overall purpose of negotiation

Discuss some options for rising health care costs

Expected product of negotiation

(Draft a table of contents for a final agreement that would be operational and durable.)

Jointly brainstorm:
   List of standards to consider
   Lists of interest
   List of options

Specific purpose of next meeting

Craft a joint recommendation for both sets of constituents

Tangible product of next meeting

(If you could imagine the piece of paper you would produce during *this* meeting, what would it contain?)

✓ A list of options for further consideration?

___ An action plan for further work necessary before an agreement would be possible?

___ A joint recommendation to your respective organizations?

___ An agreement in principle?

___ A signed contract?

___ Commitments toward the next steps?

___ Other _____

COMMITMENT 2: *Plan the Steps to Agreement*

Decision makers: names of those who will "sign" the agreement

Union president, CEO?

Implementation: information that the agreement should include about what happens next

Implementors who should perhaps be consulted before agreement is final:

Union members, Human Resources Dept., health care providers

Possible obstacles to implementation:

Rank & file might vote it down

Ways to deal with obstacles:

Lots of consultation in advance
Good explanation for result

Steps necessary to get to a binding agreement	Target date
1. Tentative agreement on issues to be included:	Done
2. Clarification of interests on each issue:	First meeting
3. Discussion of options for handling each issue:	Second meeting
4. My draft of a framework agreement:	Third meeting
5. Joint working draft of possible agreement:	30 days from now
6. Final text ready for signature:	60 days from now

A Preparation Tool Kit

Although you will not prepare for every negotiation in exactly the same way, you should have a consistent set of tools that you turn to in advance of important negotiations. Such tools would enable you to prepare systematically and efficiently for negotiations. The more you use the tools, the more effective you become at getting ready to negotiate. After a while, thinking through negotiation problems in an organized fashion becomes second nature and the tools themselves become a convenient reminder of what you should be considering.

Think of the forms in this chapter as your tool kit. Together, they provide you with a complete picture of the negotiation situation. Individually, they help you focus on specific elements of the negotiation process. Before each negotiation, flip through them and choose the ones that seem most appropriate for the situation. Remember, there are several ways you can use these forms to help you prepare:

1. You can start with the **Sudden Prep** form and decide that a limited amount of preparation is sufficient for simple, low-stakes negotiations.
2. You can use the **Priority Prep** questions to help you identify how to invest your preparation time and then use the appropriate individual form to get ready.
3. You can work through all the forms, to be prepared thoroughly for complex negotiations.

Whichever approach you choose, you may find that the first couple of times you need to refer back to the explanations and examples in the text for help with using the forms. Each chapter gives you some pointers on how to prepare well; each form helps guide you by applying those pointers to your negotiation. Consider also taking a look at **Appendix A, Getting Better at Preparation,** which works three examples through all the forms in the workbook.

Feel free to copy these blank forms as needed for your own negotiations.

INTERESTS 1: *Identify the Relevant Parties*

NEGOTIATOR: _____

COUNTERPART: _____

SUBJECT: _____

Fill in the names of the persons or groups involved in this negotiation. Put yourself as "Negotiator" and the person you are dealing with directly as "Counterpart." In the spaces below, write the names of others who may be significantly affected by the outcome of this negotiation.

People on "my side" who may care about the outcome	People on "their side" who may care about the outcome
Constituents? _____	Constituents? _____
Friends? _____	Friends? _____
Family? _____	Family? _____
Boss? _____	Boss? _____
Others? _____	Others? _____
_____	_____

INTERESTS 2: *Clarify the Interests*

Mine	Theirs	Others
What do I care about?	If I were in their shoes, what would I care or worry about?	What are the concerns of others who may be significantly affected?
Personal	**Personal**	**Other 1:**
		Other 2:
Business	**Business**	**Other 3:**

INTERESTS 3: *Probe for Underlying Interests*

NEGOTIATOR: _____

COUNTERPART: _____

SUBJECT: _____

In the left-hand column, list the more important interests for you and your counterpart that you identified on the **INTERESTS 2** form. For each of these, ask yourself "why?" and "for what purpose?" If you discover deeper interests, list them in the second column. Finally, try to rate your own interests by allocating 100 points among them in proportion to their relative importance.

Important interests (from **INTERESTS 2**)	Basic or underlying interests (Ask yourself "why?" and "for what purpose?")	Relative importance (Allocate 100 points)
Mine		
Theirs		

OPTIONS 1: *Create Options to Meet Interests*

NEGOTIATOR: _____

COUNTERPART: _____

SUBJECT: _____

Look at your **INTERESTS 3** form, then list possible ways to meet the interests on both sides. (List interests in order of their relative importance.)

My interests	Possible options	Their interests

OPTIONS 2: *Find Ways to Maximize Joint Gains*

NEGOTIATOR: _____

COUNTERPART: _____

SUBJECT: _____

Consider ways to combine skills and resources to satisfy key interests on both sides.

	Inventory of skills and resources	Combine similar resources to produce value	Combine different resources to produce value
Me			
Them			

ALTERNATIVES 1: *Think of My Alternatives to a Negotiated Agreement*

COUNTERPART: _____

SUBJECT: _____

My key interests

What could I do to satisfy my interests if we do not reach an agreement?

Possible alternatives	Pros	Cons

Of my alternatives, what will I really do if no agreement is reached (my BATNA)? Why?

What can I do to improve my BATNA? (Write down concrete steps you could take to improve your BATNA even before you go into the negotiation.)

ALTERNATIVES 3: *Identify Alternatives Open to the Other Side*

NEGOTIATOR: _____

COUNTERPART: _____

SUBJECT: _____

Their key interests

What could they do to satisfy their interests if we do not reach an agreement?

Alternatives	Pros	Cons

ALTERNATIVES 4: *Estimate Their BATNA*

NEGOTIATOR: ———————————

COUNTERPART: ———————————

SUBJECT: ———————————

What would I do in their shoes? (Which of their self-help alternatives looks best for them?)

How might I legitimately make their BATNA less attractive?

By making it harder to pursue ?	By influencing their perception of how unwise or costly it might be?

LEGITIMACY 1: *Use External Standards as a Sword and as a Shield*

What specific substantive question has to be answered in this negotiation?

Possible standards (precedents, benchmarks, prior practice, accepted principles, etc.)

Place each standard along a range from least favorable to you, to most favorable to you. Below each standard indicate what that standard would mean in this case.

Least favorable ←——————— **Standards:** ———————→ **Most favorable**

Application
of standard
to this
case:

Other standards that may be relevant or that require research:

LEGITIMACY 2: *Use the Fairness of the Process to Persuade*

Persuasive processes

If you cannot agree on an answer, you might agree on the process to find an agreeable answer. If one of the following looks interesting, how might you apply it to this case?

"I cut, you choose"

Flip a coin

Get an expert opinion

Let an arbitrator decide

The test of reciprocity

In some cases, reciprocity can be very persuasive. Are there some negotiations in which your counterpart is in a position similar to yours?

If so, what standards or arguments does he or she use in the situation?

How could you apply those standards or arguments here?

LEGITIMACY 3: *Offer Them an Attractive Way to Explain Their Decision*

NEGOTIATOR: _____

COUNTERPART: _____

SUBJECT: _____

If they had to explain the result of this negotiation to someone important to them, they could convince their constituents with the following few points:

1.

2.

3.

4.

NEGOTIATOR: _____

COUNTERPART: _____

SUBJECT: _____

The first step in dealing with your blind spots is to become aware of them. In the left-hand column, list your assumptions about their intentions and perceptions. In the right-hand column, write down key phrases your counterpart might say that should lead you to question your assumptions.

My assumptions (I assume that . . .)	Things to listen for

COMMUNICATION 2: *Reframe to Help Them Understand*

Your perspective	How might they hear it?	Reframing
(List 3–5 statements you might make to clearly put forth your interests.)	(For each statement, list your counterpart's possible response, e.g., "Yes, but . . .")	(Restate your interests so that they will hear them better.)

RELATIONSHIP 1: *Separate People Issues from Substantive Issues*

NEGOTIATOR: _____

COUNTERPART: _____

SUBJECT: _____

Describe your relationship. (Use adjectives.)

Separate the relationship from the substance

Substantive issues and problems (money, terms, dates, and conditions)	**Relationship issues and problems** (reliability, mutual acceptance, emotions, etc.)
Substantive options and remedies (Consider referring to the chapters on **Interests** and **Options**)	**Ways to improve the relationship** (Make sure these are not substantive concessions)

DATE PREPARED: _____

RELATIONSHIP 1

RELATIONSHIP 2: *Prepare to Build a Good Working Relationship*

NEGOTIATOR: _____
COUNTERPART: _____
SUBJECT: _____

What might be wrong now?	What can *I* do . . .
What might be causing any present mis-understanding?	. . . to try to understand them better?
What might be causing a lack of trust?	. . . to demonstrate my reliability?
What might be causing one or both of us to feel coerced?	. . . to put the focus on persuasion instead of coercion?
What might be causing one or both of us to feel disrespected?	. . . to show acceptance and respect?
What might be causing one or both of us to get upset?	. . . to balance emotion and reason?

Overall purpose of negotiation

Expected product of negotiation

(Draft a table of contents for a final agreement that would be operational and durable.)

Specific purpose of next meeting

Tangible product of next meeting

(If you could imagine the piece of paper you would produce during *this* meeting, what would it contain?)

____ A list of options for further consideration?

____ An action plan for further work necessary before an agreement would be possible?

____ A joint recommendation to your respective organizations?

____ An agreement in principle?

____ A signed contract?

____ Commitments toward the next steps?

____ Other _____

COMMITMENT 2: *Plan the Steps to Agreement*

NEGOTIATOR: _____

COUNTERPART: _____

SUBJECT: _____

Decision makers: names of those who will "sign" the agreement

Implementation: information that the agreement should include about what happens next

Implementors who should perhaps be consulted before agreement is final:

Possible obstacles to implementation:

Ways to deal with obstacles:

Steps necessary to get to a binding agreement   **Target date**

1. Tentative agreement on issues to be included: _____

2. Clarification of interests on each issue: _____

3. Discussion of options for handling each issue: _____

4. My draft of a framework agreement: _____

5. Joint working draft of possible agreement: _____

6. Final text ready for signature: _____

DATE PREPARED: _____   COMMITMENT 2